The Final Era:

21st Century 'Africa'!

In Breaking Down the African's Silent;

Challenges & Prediction's

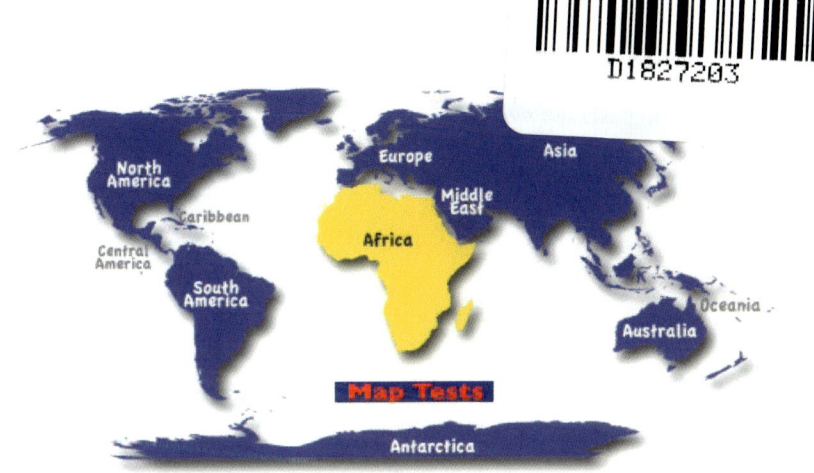

" A Unique focus on the Ethno-Political Break-down of the Africans Integration & Strength"

By

Shaibu Sunday Danladi

Shaibu Sunday Danladi

ISBN: 1500773891
ISBN-13: 9781500773892

DEDICATION

This Book is being dedicated to Enerona Shaibu whose inspiration has been so enormous in my life struggle. May you progressively work into the golden gate of intellectual's corridor with vision, determination to carry on from where I stop. So that, you too could contribute meaningfully into the society that is already degenerating for the goodness of our nations, continent and civilizations in a broad-spectrum

Shaibu JR.
Contact: Shaibu @ (dan.based@gmail.com)

Table of Contents

Ultimately, these era is an African hope and destiny to rule the world. Thus, A mission if carefully taking that could secure Africans elevation beyond being used and neglect. Therefore, All the regrettable record of Africans with regards to their historical past slave trades, colonization, scrambles and the contemporary invisible new imperialism should be an excuses for Africans not resist the future or a continuity of such evil past but it should serve as one single lessons in their hearts that should be well understood and further endure in the hearts of African youths. In order that, appropriate theory could be invented by Africans youths to fight for their eradication. Remove the bases of the misery cause by past. if it means one day, that Africans should be free from captivity. Without doubt, Africans must secure and further sustain this era which belongs to Africa advanced beyond the indebted acrobatic fabrication on their doorsteps...

Abstract:

This book attempts to clarify some of the extraordinary debate in the contemporary African continent. As well as to argue in relation to the in depth rainbow behind the historical evidences of the most African nation states miscarriage as a continent over the past decade. It further finds issues, distressing the continent underdevelopment, states of violence, poverty and the contemporary terrorism in the 21st century. Perhaps, it similarly seeks to account for some key and exact dynamics guilty for African stagnancy as weak continents despite her vast human and material wealth endowment. On the other hand, there are well-known contentment adage that we as people are breathing with an open-democratic society where every human liberty should base on a sense of balance and kept uncluttered. However, I will argue that we rather say, the universe exists as genuine, but it has been sub-changed and further sub-divided by some groups of people who had interest in Africa into a three permanent vocabulary as; (a) Taking advantage through domination (b) voluntary possession of some race (c) Invented democracy with oppression for the undeniably exploitations and radical suppression. Where is the prospect of democratic sovereignty in Africa in the 21st century?

Author`s: Book Summary;

Without a doubt, this provocative book attempts to display the new waves of the modern democratic world from the seat of African acrimonious and trauma since the decolonization of the continent during the 50s. It argues on the competences of the contemporary sovereignty in the African continent. Yet, without a doubt, it blows up numerous examples of historical documentary to enlighten how the same 'Cowboy movie world' of the past had strategically and considerably being developed in order to confine Africa beyond the knowledge of their independence despite d' so call sovereignty in the late 50s. As 'Modus operandi of symbolic trapped' to cover Africa as camp on their departure from the hands of imperials at the end of colonialism which in the contemporary time has been translated into 'African redeemer, Aid, NGO, etc. This ideological conclusion has to, in the 21st century purposefully transfer most African states into a permanent second-class inhabitant of their own continent without a passport. For instance, the period after African most celebrated independence from the late 50s was a mixed drama in the West, but with a secret maneuver to invent an ideology in the name of democratization devised at the beginning of 1990s, which had to pencil Africans into the same train as a must partner. Even so, without a portfolio for the new political ideology called democracy and African nations must be included.

There must to be democratized either by deception or violence down to this 21st century. However, to interest was this device to serve? Africans or the elsewhere colonizers? History will continue to judge on the causes of African states inadequacies. Yet, it is a fast-line technique superbly constructed from the idea of re-inventing colonization theology. African youth must watch-out!

These elevated instruments had to permanently shift the entire African continent confidence and the rest of the under develop world through logic, trick policy, ideas privately calculated and framed at all-embracing democracy after decolonization. The plausible features of the book are that it questions under what role or constitutions made democracy a universal identity. As the policies of this idea are politically invented under the canopy of the West, which is not different from the legacy of imperialism in Africa and the rest of the world. In this book, such ideas as the universality of democratization, including Africa is what I will designate as *'white dove without a feather''* a method developed to shorten African exit, escape from their un-ending transition from dependency by the Western nations. This book also notes that, the plan to separate each Western country's airport into 'Third countries; Schengen countries, Asian countries, etc. have to indicate a strategic commitment by the 'West' to promote a true separation from the other world on the spirit of inequality by race, etc. However, while at African's airport such disparities are not grounded in the African continent airports nor do not and will never exist. This kind of approach has to in a larger appendage had to cut off the uniqueness and sincerity of unity among people and their conviction towards one supreme universal order as democratization towards integration, oneness, and unity of purpose in these worlds as those who constructed the image name democracy may require us to know. Nevertheless, I will suggest that if 'democracy' true spirit exists elsewhere, To be sure, in reality, to harmonize humanity integration, I will refer such ideas of democracy as *strategic theory of exploitation* instead of an idea invented for human liberty and freedom. So, how radically strong and accuracy can this book launch into intellectual and human history a new knowledge is born? A must-read book in the 21st century (Shaibu 2011)

The 21st Century engagement in Africa;

'In pursuit of unthinkable survival'?

Democratization in Africa Nation States; Upsurge of New Civilization in Africa'?

" It is not about 'we are trying' it is about challenging the faces of our politics, policies, strategies and logics with a realistic demand beyond transformation, but to search a right direction to sustainable stability, development, integration to escaping the historical inadequacies fabricated into our continent. We neither challenge this root causes of *our history itself, nor perish in instability, poverty, dependency and violent we both help preserve or even established" (Shaibu, 30th 11/2013)*

Introduction:

The experience of the African nation's decade after the continent eventual promising independence from the late 50s has been challenging. Faced with unceasing instability and democratic uncertainties, scholars had sub-charge their intellectual understanding towards the complexities facing Africa continent with different views over the past centuries without a specific recommendation, which defines the difficulties the continent faces in the span of years. This shortcoming has drawn attention to African scholars to analytically pre-empty the contemporary enigma in the continent of Africa. It must also be grouped among other things which majority of Europeans had proper solutions to the challenges African state faces. However, it may be possible to say that none of these remarks is intended to remove the ultimate responsibilities for developing African from the shoulder of the African peoples. Not only are there African accomplices inside the imperialist system, but every African has a responsibility to comprehend the system and to work to eliminate its over-throw[1].

---

[1]

See, Walter Rodney, How Europe underdeveloped Africa, and an Introduction by

This ultimate responsibility may have signaled the key genetic root for assembling this book for the continued elevation of African political and institutional developments by challenging every problem the countries in African faces without biases nor blind faith to protect some interest against the will of African people. The imaginary of the contemporary African smuggle into an undeniable state of uncertainties may have not been too distance from the continent inability to re-define the recorded challenges of the continent. Therefore, as long as such demanding questions are leftward unturned, the situation in Africa will continues to be validated itself in African political institutions. In this inquiry, African history had a burden within African societies and people, and those burdens are peculiar to the realities African faced today as undeniable political struggles for survival. Where could African start their search for political and institutional realities? This explosive question is vigorously answered in the context of this whole book. Africa must establish an organ, which does not fear from storms and must be ready to stand on a new track for a sustainable development and possibly on a grounded search for their own national realities instead of keeping forging together in darkness without peace and unity among the fabricated institutions (Shaibu, Jan. 2014).

Vincent Harding. 1982, Pp. Xii-xxi,

The first chapter of this radical book contributes to the revolutionary questions that is facing many states in the African continent today stretching from which direction possible could allow the fabricated countries in the African continent to survive the 21st century.

Democratization In Africa Continent;

'The upsurge of new civilization'
Supremacy As 'Democratic Order into Africa?

> *"My history was changed and further caged even before I was born a man. Our parents were made to serve under the unknown king outside our land of origin and culture. How should my next generation be governed under the same unknown and purposeless continents? We are made to believe we are less human with values in our own land. My heart is broken" (Shaibu, 2013, 03,25th; 1; 25am)*

Africa; how it all started>

Stage 1;

Historically, one may perhaps say, the expedition of the African continent over a number of decades of their separate independence could be shortened in a single word "Confusion". The entire African leaders in both past and present may even attempt to disprove this indication, but this is the full stock of the countries in Africa as fact. The question now is 'how can African start their journey into the 21st century new moon blinking with many facts about the African unrealistic journey over the years? I am quite sure many intellectuals will try to question my brilliant effort to uncover the state of Africa fluctuation and confused state of the democratic journey since decolonization. Still, A child at thirty-seven years now could not be called boy rather but a man who as witness little good and evil of this generation given his experiences and research. Now here we are alone together. Africans fast losing the trail of their abundance is not a matter of historical distortion alone, but there is a lot of concern about what African has made with their sovereignty in the past century. Consider, for instance, an African pan-water aid manager report recently, and I quote; " 330 million Africans today live without access to fresh water, so the route to travel is long, but we can for the first time sees the end in the sights" Mr F. He also went further to argue that Africans will not accept failure'. In the real science of knowledge about the failures of Africa over the last decades could simply means that, the most significant problems in African sovereign states over development and change in Africa often sound like a dream to African elites, no wonder there will never believe any commentary about the reality of their failures. But issues relating to distributing equal access to public institutions is reflected in elites mind as difficult and in some instances impossible to achieve forgetting that an organized thinker with a global claim to justice will earn Africans more than they identify justification as 'reforms' could ever present to the continent. We may as a matter of policy, consider 'a group is not perceived as a constructive part of the political community if it is denied that status in the public domain which other groups do enjoy as a matter of course. It is quite obvious that the Africans were disorganized and further exploited to the highest pedigree by the Europeans in their scramble for wealth, economic benefits and cheap labour, but while we may call many of these stories as history, what effect has those histories contribute to changing Africa political landscape?. The contemporary stages of a new wave of domination in Africa and the emerging face of imperialism worth the judgment of our time. There has been a persistent reservation towards African by Europeans after decolonization, which could only be assumed from the European indirect calculation to resist Africans significant knowledge of their histo-traditions, and knowledge through the West calculated belief for democratic legitimacy as the only ways to efficiency in Africa. Nevertheless, the changing of imperialistic interpretation and the new face of imperialism is awesome and quite logical that have to use African politicians against themselves by using different kind of tricks to legalize their priority in Africa. To be sure, why should Africa be place like 'status with only one strain of political definition of states? This is to say the entire African continents were made to adopt a kind of presidential political logic as appropriate for political representation which is to help resolve African from division but forcing their integration as one nation. This view as quite false prophesies against African stability. This process of legitimacy as a presidential system of government, which empower a particular individual as both head of states and government have to make the African continents president so powerful that corruption, repression, oppression, nepotism, inadequacies and stick could be used to carry on exploiting the continents from generation to posterity. Thus, the states of violence, criminal killings, political and institutional manipulation enforce and protect as legitimate etc. all this motivate has to contribute to the contemporary states of African states of confusion and continuing exploitations by a different formal imperial lord for their benefits and coast-to-coast interest. Let's consider this point, how did democracy contribute to leading African into a kind of imagining growth in the next 100 years as claimed by the Western ideology? Of course, any general sensible individual will suggest that the future of Africa will never be forecast from the states of their modern existence as democratic societies because there were not instituted on a legal, structural, civil, social, environmental, climate, linguistic consideration, and regionalism and according to their local needs nor community understanding in line with their cultural values and traditions. Here we may say, justice requires us, However, that we African's consider sharing the challenges of our diminishing from the global relevance, acknowledge the legacies and the benefits of our historical burden of slave trade, colonialism, exploitations and even those we 'our self-created without common knowledge and motive behind the long term implication for such actions. What makes African integration as one solid project in most cases fail in cooperation among each other is because African states do not seem to think on equal term as people of the same race and until such undertaking are recognized by African and further sanctions, the possibility to having equal states of mind as citizens of the continent as well as living under one legal institution as our own sovereign nations with purposeful stability will often be like a

4

night dreams. What is virtually the legitimate status as we both live as African's know about ourselves as our options?. This view to a great astonishing, fail to make any reasonable contribution to the African ideas of foreign policy, nor as measures to African strategic moves to advance the status of the countries in Africa from peril. It is not more news that Africa had almost tried every ideology from the Western world as a means to their economic recovery from anarchy and chaos over the past decade. However, the image of stability in Africa seems to continue changing identity, tradition, prospect and climate and the advantages have never been in African people and states of affairs. Why should securing a convincing control of African ground engagement with sustainability have been very difficult and even impossible? What deprived African from escaping the exploitation, distortions and states of hazard regions been claimed over by wars, violence, crime, terrorism and constant non-recognition by the international communities within heavy weight resourceful wealth? Many points may have contributed to this autonomous definition of failures, as we shall discuss in the following section

Stage 2

The Expansionism Towards Africa: 'You Lead We Control You'

'We know at least one attempt'

The answer for the above expression might not be speedy, but it will prove to be efficient in accounting for the position of African states being vanquished by the Western domination, influence on the African economic strategy leading to the contemporary emerging new waves of exploitations into Africa. There is a tendency we start at looking at interstate conflict and states of violence in African continents. For examples, African elites have been engaged in ever increasing high rate of insecurity apparatus since decolonization, as others will claim that, it is an attempt to resist any rebel attack by the existing state. This claim in Africa is quite a notion with different explanations. First, in an attempt to meet the society demand as minority and majority does not involve only on redistribution of political power among nor within regions, but in real and practical logic, it demands a re-designed of the institutional outlook of the society. This could be done either by re-organized the groups of regions invented by imperialism or by total elimination of the entire framework. Shifting to some extent all kinds of development ideas into building a legal, structural institutions under a sound negotiation and agreements. Where

African elites who want to radically improve Africa do not conceive such ideas, it comes to means recycling the invented states of anarchy left by the imperial master's decade ago. Perhaps, issues of African failures have been hashed out, presented and continue to question over the past decades yet, the precious lord of development and stability seem to be far from African reach despite much outcry from both the minority, the less privilege and those placed under compulsory dependency and poverty created by the emerging African elites to head African empires. What are the different between imperialist and Africa leaders after a long history of sovereignty in Africa? Indeed, it is not more a fact in Africa that the continent had lost her authority over sovereignty a struggle that brought much life to attain to a mere selfish interest and corruption of deceit through a careful Western strategic manipulation of African's with different as policy towards safeguarding Africans stability. The trick here altogether is to continue expanding European industrial outlet for importation of armaments and weapons from European to continue defending their 'holding tight to power over the people. To be sure, African continent today have to become a fast growing market or European weaponry market to many Africans to buy weapons and be killing their next generation and old once in the name of politics, rebels, enemy of the states, terrorism. Likewise, we could observe the increasing deployment of Europeans military to engage in African civil society for secretly and careful design approach to removing some African oppositions to government through any possible method define by in the name protection against unknown rebels. So, the African country becomes home for both light weapons and machinery for killing rebels, the blood keeping oozing out from the vine of African premature killed in the name of saving regime while the industries manufacturing them gain and benefits from another wave of expansion into Africa. In most cases, the justification for all this superior is to hold Africa elites as lack of vision for their people. How funny will this situation sound-Yet? This is the true face of African reality over the years. We may also point at various histories of constitutional framework embark by different regions of Africa over several years, but no one could claim to be efficient enough as compared to numerous countries around the world spring out from their colonial heritage in getting hold of their sovereignty. If Africa missing something tangible about their relevance in the world politics? Sometimes, I often think that African leaders really need to pause and reflect on the journey so far about their historical and contemporary network of failures designing, shaping and re-shaping or even at re-interpretations of re-imperialism with their wide eyes open without even having the knowledge of what is missing within the continent as brown race people. Africa must re-group to secure themselves from captivity in the 21st century. An issue that worth a calculative rethinking towards devising a stability treaty for African societies and people.

Stage 3

Africa A Distress of Africa Political History:
End Of Braved Diplomacy Into Africa Possible?

Global Crisis; Issues with respect to the African continent in the 21st century present to us what a political scientist could refer as 'crisis of political and diplomatic miscalculation' in Africa. This and other event had to establish such a faster shift towards another world war III in Africa through diplomacy. Perhaps, we could even say, "No Great leader in history fought to prevent change," Said... Maxwell, J. C... However, I often imagine with heartbreaking how society holds tight to antiquity character unchanged'. Is something missing with our generation leaders in Africa"... Shaibu Sunday Danladi, 2013) it is no longer news that, over the last phase of the decade, countries around the world have been struggling with various shifting cultivation of ideas and policies towards sovereignty, autonomy, sustainability with different mindsets. Specifically to African's. No doubt, on one side the story is clear as some countries are striving to maintain their social and human being to be sovereign nations, e.g. Iranians, Syrians, North Koreans, Congo, etc. And on the other path, other nations are struggling to escape from the leading remote controlling devices being placed constantly on their right and freedom by questioning about accepting democratic transitions as the only messiah backed from the Western ideology that could afford the entire global world stability and functionality. But, how valid is the alternative views are somewhat mysterious to many intellectuals around the world order. For instance, as we have witnessed the democratic transition in Iraq, Afghanistan, Egyptian's revolutions, Libya, Tunisian, and the ongoing war currently in Syria. The idea of democracy here may have a hint different agenda instead creating states of stability in several countries mentioned above. Even so, No single bureaucratic countries are quite obviously of the fading ideological traps setting up around the globe from the West. Do we live in a mars? Why has human ideas never learn a lesson from its failures and chaotic suffering of people in pains? However, the pressure to construct the whole world as democracies hardly ceased from the heart of those Western countries on creating democratic transitions. Let's us look closely to some key unforgettable wars, distortions in innocent children's put to deaths by our collective actions, miseries and hardship we launch into another nation's sovereignty, and many others we have helped to destruction and collapsed in the past. What sort of evidence could explain the guilty of our destructive policies towards other countries and continents? We are all aware that many of these projects we were involved for decades have failed us wholly without any particular visible achievements worth remembering in human memory. How can the collective world system change into democratic oppression where the world is made up of particular human creed, culture, traditions, beliefs, and social ways of life? It is more of reality than being a mere fact that the world systems are different and can never be the same because we must use different views in different terms geographically from one continent to another to pull this unpretentious investigation. Some country like Mali is a landlocked country, no sea and the weather conditions are extremely harsh during the summer period. Czech Republic is not blessed with gold nor crude oil, but by tourism, taxes, penalties, technological industries, etc. It generates from the few sources she was conferred by nature, China's success as the modern world largest and prosperous economic system is not democratic countries, but could give her industrial revolutions above that of many Western democratic nations. Congo has diamond, gold and many other viable resources that if properly develop could build another haven in Africa sub-regions, but the combined shared greed's of humanity would not allow seeing Congo progression beyond dependency. Therefore, as we have seen from the little geopolitical calculations, each region, countries, continents achieves higher from several domestic policies invented locally to support their growth and maturation. This is not about democratic transitions; it is about sustainability of society by delivery of every social amenity needed by the people. Fundamentally, many indications from history have proven us wrong that we are not doing the right things specifically to Africans. Nevertheless, here we are doing the same thing from generation after another without change of neither theory nor idea towards encouraging sustainable societies especially to Africa. While the relevant development agenda had been suspended by Western countries towards Africa over the past decade in both colonial era and post colonial subjugations, here we are, still very much presenting facts and figures of financial aids, donating weapons to crisis regions of our interest in Africa. Yet, the extraordinary issues of African realistic stability are entirely been suspended and further neglected. Should Africa believe the Western countries are singing to African people with different fine turn voices? Yes!. It is quite true about the Western diplomacy over the years in Africa. Even so, the most interesting questions is that, 'are we really saying the truth about the African continent with the exactness our mind as people of honesty and concern about Africa continent and people? No! As W. G. Bush radically proclaimed during the 2000 presidential inauguration campaign, he issued one undeniable proclivity of the Western countries in African continent when he alleged, I in particular, dismissed Africa as being a part of the world where the US had no real interests. This suggests under the spontaneous ideology shaping several Western countries about Africa. Then, why should the ideas of Western democracy be relevant to the African continent as one and the only messiah to deliver African continent into sustainability and prosperity? From here, we could recognize that African is such a coaching ground like children playing soil for the Western countries. Let's use them and dump them. We have no interest about children without senses. A message well-tailored and clearly understood by the 21st African youths on the path to their own liberty. On the other hand, as we could underpin from the historical antecedent of Africa continents with a unique reflection on the 21st century, especially over the last 15 years until the date, the emerging powers had to make it clear and significantly trying to triumphs over the negligence of the Western diplomacy and political deceptions to navigate into the African heartland full of potentially, Economic abundance, wealth, Minerals, and its dominance in terms of the largest green land in the world for the business and in return, Africa is getting the needed attention through advance in development, industry, market, technology, etc. This mark the ends of imperial era by the Western diplomacy in Africa which I believed the West should obviously adhere and further accept the situation as it keeps unfolding so that Africa could be developed to meet its people and regions all the essential attention and stability of purpose the continent needed and has being lingering decade after post-colonialism.

Stages 4

Re-modification of mindset into Africa:
Any Decent Word Possible?:

'The Western Economic crisis vs. the African economic growth

As mentioned earlier, the sustainability of any nation's growth does not depend on global democratic salvation, but domestic strategic approach towards stability by the indigenous nation states. Contrary, as we could observe from the various Western countries deeply face with the increasing global economic challenges, depreciation and further crisis, which indeed, has, being driving theses nations along a lonely path of the paradise in 21st century. Perhaps, we could likewise say, that the circumstances tripping the Western remarkable capitalist economic legitimacy, climate and environmental redefinition is a smart challenges seeking changes across Europe. It is quite striking that this contests worth a unique lessons to be learn from these diverse catastrophe, and it is fair, we consider the state of affairs as a clear indication that the European predicament is a signal to the Western institutional miscarriages as to their vast hegemonic supremacy. Therefore, I will suggest that the success of the world stability could be a straightforward mathematical calculation, which is to accept the challenges that is shaping our all-encompassing societies around us. Perhaps, the challenge is to break-down our Western preserve effort, laws in constructing various boundaries around human societies, integrations and stability. The most outrageous complicated gaps invented in international politics as *we must lead them* policies often fabricated into the world politics to cover the faces of reality on the ground, under which the making of instabilities around the axis of the globe are being recognized and preserved for serving groups of personalities, countries and continent around the world (Shaibu, 14th March 2014). More likely, we may also wish to visualized the future with the previous history of the past, reflecting on some key issues of inconsistencies of human inadequacies and miseries over the earlier decade. It should be tailored in such a way that the present and the near future would worth a rethinking as significant obstacle to be tackle with a courage to comprehend their impacts on human civilization. So that strategic dialogue concerning a stable economic, political, social states of both Africa, Asia and European economic collapsed is recognize and as well brought forward and treated collectively so that the entire world could steer a booming economy and political stability without diplomacy. The issues of Western diplomacy across global societies has been properly recognized by many nations, continent and as well well preserved with both hatred and pains over an issues of taking advantage over the misery causes by the Western cruel reaction to many nations' internal affairs. The creations of wars, hunger, poverty, devastation and hopelessness engineered by these global cruel economic demand over many decade has being of a greater damages in both chaos, wars, conflict and terrorism around the world. This view is very much well acknowledge around the international affairs. Yet, nothing significant give the impression worth doing something tangible about it. Given the several human refugees in every Conner of our societies. For instance, Wang Jisi, of Beijing University, has observed that "many developing countries that have introduced Western values and political systems are experiencing disorder and chaos" and that China offers an alternative model. Countries from Africa (Rwanda) to the Middle East (Dubai) to South-East Asia (Vietnam) are taking this advice seriously[2]. I will argue that until people and their cultures are allowed to live in their opinions, men's and their environments collectively relates with each other without double game's theories for their existence, sovereignty and their sustainability are allowed to be cultivated without political and propagate threats against those regions. Any form of creative possibilities of safety in this world will be short of being answered. What, indeed, therefore, are good options for democratic transitions if another human being's freedoms to survive are being treated consistently of war or through political deceptions? I am quite aware of history that until the Western claims and continued search for global dominance in

2

See, the economics, what is wrong with the democracy? http://www.economist.com/news/essays/21596796-democracy-was-most-successful-political-idea-20th-century-why-has-it-run-trouble-and-what-can-be-do controlling the whole world remotely is being broken, either by those countries of the West themselves or their countries will be forced to collapse through their involvement in other countries, continents of the world, the world will hardly be a better place of peace and harmony in human history (Shaibu, 2014-Prague). At this useful dimension, (J.W. Smith, 2000) suggests that "Only after one understands how freedom and rights are being oppressed by the managers of imperial states — even as they preach peace, freedom, justice, rights, and majority rule to their citizens to defend their beliefs in the morality of their society, and therefore ensure the continued sustenance of the masses for inflicting such violence upon the cosmos — can one write honest history. If one does not understand that process, one is almost sure to compose a history in which, unbeknownst to the author, the background and documentation have been carefully created to give Managers of State the freedom to conquer other people's rights and transfer their wealth to the imperial centre through unequal trades"1. We are now living in democratic gangsters as we may conclude the section that, the entire unpredictability of the global power shift will be an end to several Western diplomacy. We should as a matter of fact note that, we are all part of the world instability, we know it, and we must adopt to modify our policies. Else, violence and wars, poverty and destitution, poverty and miseries, the global and cultural uncertainty we have devised. We may as a process look at it differently. When shall be occasion for universal change to see the world the ways it? In order not to gamble with these scholarly contributions presented here, the time is ripped enough for the global society should be painted from the domestic value of geopolitical interpretations rather from than from the abstracts of Western   values   alone.

Stage 5

The Half-baked Global Politics Towards Africa.
Why African States Are Fragile And Crumbling?

Is Africa Liberty & Freedom Suspended Already?

African countries, as many of us are doubtless familiar with it from each of our individual countries of the world, from every corner of human race as leaders, etc. if we search critically, we will acknowledge from our deepest honest imagination that the so called 'problems of the Africans' are not in any realistic and accepted calculative as accurate African people created predicaments. So far, whether we imagine it or not, a number of problems challenging the African continent today originate from those fabricated neither directly nor indirectly from some external forces through more or less consistent and calculated deceptions from both West and the repose of the contemporary emerging powers in the African sub-neighborhoods. Indeed, most of this illustration and fabricated thoughts by deception with active propaganda historically, artificial report about various spots that had never existed within African people being forceful and calculated by some unarmed element to facilitate pro-long dependency of African people over the long time. Yet, how more long time should Africans keep crumbling behind a Western ideological tactician? Conceivably, it is rather striking for one to observe how poverty is being witnessed in Africa by groups of men whose effort is to device blueprint by men and woman of external power and interest in Africa continent in both during the slave trade, direct colonialism and at post-colonialism under which African continents still being put into its modern decays. No doubt, Africans were today impressively left alone to sew their own ignorance as children, which not at any time wants to grow beyond dependency from the Western capitalist economy. Even so, I repeatedly consider various forces deceiving African integration and stability as those superficially design projections for African people as that race which lack adequate moral thought about what freedom means to their own people, values, identity. Yet, the issues of universal laws using a device of democratization becomes a fundament tools for the new waves of re-exploitation of Africa continent and elsewhere in a strait Jacket. Supplementary, beyond so much celebrated democracy, which does not respect human right, liberty and freedom to dwell in the land of the freewheel from God. Nevertheless, to those of us whose personalities are to produce a calculation to ignite a continual war in the entire world, paving ways to the constant anarchy and the destruction of compassionate freedom by wars for the benefit of those artificially personal aggrandizements is such a painful vision in the world we dwell today. *It`s fundamental, correct, we recognized that Africans* *people in an independence struggle had to drop off discriminatory difference connected with their dissimilarities, language, regions, but to fight a collective shift by recognizing themselves as African only to seek an avenue to secure themselves a permanent release from the chain of destructions call area of influences which was designed to permanently set African into backwardness and dependency since (1884-85).* Once more, several years after such a dreadful map up of Europeans to frustrate African liberty fails and most African countries gain their independence of which some made it through violence, E.g., Algeria to be specific, Ethiopia However, without a formal colonial settlement were not easy as well. Nevertheless, the Italian indirectly and strategically ruler fueled wars of interest in Ethiopia, through Eritrea which started from 1890- 1936 up until to end when Eritrea secure their independence in 1993 from Ethiopia. However, during the Italian quest to dominate and further control Ethiopia's kingdom, which later failed several ethnic violence to get Eritrea separated from Ethiopia. However, in another similar occasion, Ghana got freedom from the British in 1957, Nigeria 1960s, and Cameroon 1961 and so on. Conversely, today, directs colonization has finally been resolved and further buried politically. Nevertheless, strategically, Africans continent is very much been considered under a chain of cunning ideas of the Western assembly tactics through a mechanizing democratic manipulations to the entire nations of the world. On the contrary, how many African continent are technically free today from the previous colonial grip on the

Africa are considerable left on the fence of politics to be questioned. Then, it should be a garden-fresh and wide exposed that everyone with insight about Africa possibly will know that Africans are still combatting with the uncertainties created in the past and with the developing reality on the emerging powers into Africa. Indeed, it should be clear from the foregoing that several journey into Africa by different countries are not likely for the development of the continent rather for the goodness of their domestic people back home while helping in frustrating the African continent growth, expectation and development beyond dependency. Even so, currently, what is hanging on the Africa sleeve is how to live on and penetrate Deeping the development of their entire regions respectively. For such a move, in Nov. 2011, Several religious leaders of African regions turn to Turkey Istanbul to discussing the most African Deeping crises which were called 'Africans problems can be solved with Turkey-led commission' were thoughtful African leaders which was led by Malian Islamic president Mahmoud Dikko and was attended by forty-six Africans countries respectively. Though, most one hundred and twenty-five countries were in attendance. It may interest us to know also that, the entire vision in this forum are those technically support about how to set effort to secure Africans peace and stability. Like the rest of a number of delegates, Mr. Diko, trace that Africans problem, he notes ""Our troubles are non-religious. We have very complex, interwoven problems. But, the issue is weapons in most of the African countries. To sustain a platform in our future together, a powerful country like Turkey needs to take the platform." While also in response to Mr. Dikos comments, Djibouti Republic's religious affairs Hahmoud reinstates "Islamic state are experiencing mental confusion. Natural disasters can be overcome, but there does not appear to be an easy solution to the problems resulting from sect differences and internal conflicts." At this very beginning, to confront two idealist position of the Africans leaders mention above, it should be made efficiently clear that as Greek philosophers would often say, that political justices are an imposition of human ideas, and not a reflection of natural justices[3] and this view may perhaps even mandate us to a belief that most African country's predicaments are not those elements of fabricated Western media reports, but those set from the outside calculated puzzle towards creating an unjust level of confusion in the African continents by the so called area of interest. For instance, the largest amount of advance light weapon's, Dreadful weapons of mass destruction quickly found its way into the African continent in the names of defending insecurity and instability in the Africa from the hands of rebels. Who are actually the African rebels causing wars, conflicts, riots around the globe peace existence? I believe we are all known what I am talking about. Certainly, we are all involved in setting Africa states into

---

[3]

    See Plato, (427-347 BCE) ancient political thoughts. The politics book, pp37, 2013)

instability by the name of our collective interest without considering the implication such interest might plan for other country stages of uncertainty. When shall we differentiate the goals of stability, instability and insecurity we both establish as dramatic strategy through deceptions, we create from other countries, even in the faces of our artificial drafted democratic relevance? I will propose that the position taken by the Western world to influence the idea of universality of democratic theory, which its crucial code definition is that 'every country must be democratized is absolutely radical and further questionable. Possibly, in my own intellectual taking, 'democratic theory' should be discarded from all axis of human endeavor (Shaibu, 16th March 2014) this observation suggests that from the angle, I look at the constant emerging conflict around the world today is being led by ideas of what I often term *'democratic devilism towards Africa'* shaking people and their states into anarchy, poverty and total separation and even in most cases into destruction being advanced by our deception. Though, I will admit that we should allow institutions, states, regions and continent decide what there want, how they want their countries be organized in a peaceful atmosphere, ruled nor govern themselves. This is the most important of the law of nature. Especially when looked from the nativity of our kids. Our kids did not decided were to be born, when to be born, regions to be born and continents without states neither president nor capitalism groups telling a pregnant woman where her child must be born or how he or she should be born while very much in the womb etc. I mean, people and their nation's, groups of identity who belong together historically should be allowed to find their basic natural liberty through re-union according to their past. To create their own territory where they find fit they could live with their human liberty and freedom guaranteed instead of those *'we often design for people outside our continent' who make us a prophet of salvation in a free society of mankind*? Design by an autocratic and complex artificial democratic commission. For instance, religious faith is such a free institution where everyone owns the autonomy to select where to go without anyone pushing you into it. So, countries and their people should be freely released by the international capitalism's design, cosmopolitan laws to secede and live with freedoms without groups of interest pursuing them because of their own self-aggrandizement. I confidently believe that the contemporary African continent must stand up to lead a fight to take down the problematic institution's design and protected by the international laws for the vulgar pastime of some groups of countries and bags. Particularly if scrutinized from the Western axis of calculation towards the Africa continent concretely. On the status of decays in Africa as often proclaimed by the West that African continent needed West if not they will almost immediately collapse as a continent. This is one magic which may bend our attention to what the future of Africa considerably... look like, beyond the expected by the Western world. Insightfully, Let the West 'Remove their aids to Africa, remove their troops in some strategic countries in Africa, draw back their financial support to Africa and try to avoid Africa completely for one year and let's examine who will stomach aches from the needs of the African wealth's? Every state needs another for one design or the other by strengthening each other towards development and escaping ranges of poverty and destitution, but back to African people, most Western countries beliefs 'it is not our interest' to do this, but we only need their resources. If so, why not take the resources, but stop fueling violence and instability to already disorganized institution you both artificially design, which had to initiate a capital offensive to African people as one unforgettable source of suffering in the Africa continent. What had the African people gained from the Western brainwashing since post-colonialism if not a track record of re-imperial design policies to continually tricking the Africans continent into a Western multi-national door-post as dependency continent? Coincidentally, the future of African integration, advancement beyond dependency on the Western calculated democratic tactics, stability and viable liberty for the African posterity lies in the political program, which could account for citizenry and society re-union and further creating industrial output for the nation's liberty from dependency. This position if properly taking into caution, several messages from African history are very much a painful outlook which had no single peaceful legacies for African youth posterity. Why should Africa not face the challenges of breaking these radical traps of poverty, violence, lack of integration, pretended and illegal boundaries constructed for them so that Africa could initiate and design another perfect Map for African people by themselves? May we perhaps even check with the following accession which tries to question 'why several transitions in Africa could not establish a relief to already fragile society by bringing forward a plausible path to African Salvation through development and stability? I will contend that political platform which embodied African instability has been sentenced to a outlook and further to starve through ideological and group's sanctions by both internal and external self-aggrandizement against the will of African people. I should further put forward that the only survival of the African people, liberty and freedom from the externally crafted deception in Africa is that African people most design an alternative modern of policies towards their own survival and to neglect nor even ignored any form of crafted jointly ideas to facilitate African people against their own peoples as rebels to say. In my own consent to say, Africa must acknowledge that an epoch often comes and go. Just as the entire world is experiencing a global changing and geopolitical shifting currently. Therefore, the epoch of the Western diplomacy in Africa continent through an officially design network has expired in Africa long ago. I should suggest Africa people should live with this observation as piece of evidence to press ahead in taking charge as the supremacy and prophet over their own continent, resources, countries and citizenry irrespective of culture, traditions or regionalism. This epoch is an

Africa era for advancement beyond depending on the Western world. The liberty for African people is, set their path to freedom by liberating every corner of African people from the muddle of their historical records of accomplishment. By this token, the project in Africa is to recognize the needs for their own particular method of nationhood that could eventually lead them to escape the pretended chain of imperialism disabling the advancement of the African continent. Doubtless, as we have witnessed over the various parts of this book, many promises of democratic uniqueness to African continent have been those designs with contradictory messages, which has being in a sharp contrast with reality on solving the so called African continent. In bringing too close to Africa issues, the extraordinary land of the African continent as hand of hope will continue to last in prosperity. The only thing I could visualize is that African people must actively stand to get organized, get-together to be in command of their own continent from the hands of predators. Who has had no stake in preserving Africa, developing Africa as equal in partnership, even in a dream in order to seize an opportunity to promote their individual progression by challenging every deposited design handicap sinking African states into decays and anarchy before the close of the 21st century?

What, However, we should learn from this era of 21st centuries is that, Africans recognize that it is in this era that the wheel of driving Africa sub-region sustainability shall be specified. At peak, this determining optimism is such a test in the face of global affairs on how African people had quietly comes to recognize what liberty certainly means as to get rid of its causes of dependency. Equally well, the youths of Africa are running hard to secure their posterity released from the hands that had since the dark ages initiate a sort of limit on Africans developmental progress. A technique, which has succeeded by, suspended the capable, sincere minds of Africans liberty for decades. Insightfully, Africans are striving to seek mastery of their own safeguarding future and fulfilment. Without unrestrained forces from the external network to smuggle African society once more from exploiting their own liberty. While today's Africans intellectual is obviously looking beyond the past and had already endured enough to get ahead for a prosperous progress of their next generation of African posterities. For that reason, Africans must and had equally acknowledged clearly that their liberty, development, escape from poverty, dependency matters to them more than gold. Africans liberty, Sovereignty in my own intellectual judgment is not for sale, but from each generation, the questions of equality will go forward to be taken by the Africans offspring's while also trying to by working together in order to get rid of all vestiges of imperial contradictory, tricky policies from the outdoor world for their domestic survival. A course to position Africa on a conduit of a democratization transition that is pure, pairs with equal liberty, development with a courage is what linked objectivity with pathways to salvation real (Shaibu, Dec.2014)

Stages Six:

The African Challenges:

Is Africans survival conceivable?

It may has being insincerely garnish from the past decade of the continent of African by the elsewhere colonizers as African nations would never be able to delineate themselves without the Western nation. Yet, but as centuries passed into the contemporary globalization, most such Western thoughtful authenticities as the true God-father for the African survival had been put to question as to what nourishes the West believe that there has absolute dominion over the African continent, people and societies only as tools for their own survival? Historically, The African enslavement, which began around the 16th century by the West, continues to hold Africans into captivity through a best-known trade as triangular system where Africans were sub-changed for goods and service during the dark ages. It then comes the end of the slave of trading when the French government decided to put an end to their quest for slave trading in 1794 as the first European to establish such a determination to stop the inhuman trading of Africans as commodities. African people and their freedom as a human race continue to undergo such a harsh treatment in the hands of the West until around 1848 when the slave trade was formally abrogated. However, the trading of human captives,

Especially of African origins continues to come out in a dissimilar facet as a wholesale civilization by the Europeans with various wiles policies, democratization and trade rules. While in 21st centuries, aid to Africans and essentially a form of borrowing of finances as cash to African's countries with a heavy tax attached to this effect, which had to repeatedly shifting African states under the European remote regulator... We may also remember vividly that the European interest in the continents of Africa through a direct colonization which eventually started around 1814 by the British when there snatched the Dutch protectorate in the southern African and further decided to demarcate every region into their possession. Even so, The other Europeans were equally important not excluded as the French, Portuguese, Belgium, Dutch and Germans quickly stretching their fingers to grab the green lands of hope in the African continent which had to continue to date despite African's country's independence since 1960s. Thus, despite the end of such an acrimonious interest of the 19th centuries from Botswana to Namibia, Southern Africa, most African countries continue to be the subject of European political control through their foreign policy networks. Perhaps, neither does the close of the 20th century could be forgotten without mentioning the Western grabs on the African continents. Especially as the British hold's Egyptian firmly to the ends of the twentieth century. As many of us could see today, African continents remain one of the backward continents in human history of civilization? Does this situation reflect that the journey of the West in civilizing African continents a realistic project? For instance, Between the 1920s and 1975 when Angola was eventually free to allow them to join other independent African countries, the story behind the marine's interest of the West in Africa continues to steer much African nation's stability through different movements towards African people. This is a stage where we can immediately view the majority of Africans been detained to forceful occupation by the Western forces, especially that of the United Nation in Congo since 1961 without being able to procure a peace treaty in Congo democratic Republic. What is going exactly on the international laws? Indeed, the consistently demands of the African economically wealthy are to be the fair one of the reason's where African stability can never be sustainable until the African people stand against the West policies towards Africa continent. Although, while the majority of the African continents lead the world in high levels of the poverty ratio, the questions on how does scores of nations in the African continent found themselves in such a dreadful situation had to be suppressed and strictly not at any time to be clearly determined by both the West and their collaborator's African leaders. Today, the economy of African continent continues to grow in both size and weight. Which implies that Africa significant position in the world politics cannot longer be ignored? How does the West actually try to reconcile the past different ideas there successfully established to keep African countries under their remote resistor? The planet of African potential had every tendency to satisfy the demands of the world food, survival, but how can the un-ending conflict of interest to African people be neither explained nor rather rectified to give many Africa people a chance to dominate the world? We may see today as every indication had provided us that African continent had shifted their faith and direction of guidance from the West tactical politics in the course of African 21st century demand to break up the past economy's substance depend on the West. Therefore, The many wealth in Africa today and its growth has indicated a shift of power in Africa and not even Asia as most scholars had earlier suggested. Africa is a hub under which the world stability of food, energy, and mineral resources is deposited and preserved naturally. And the other nations cannot do any substantial foreign policy without Africa. However, Africa is not important to us. Who controls the voices of false hold in Africa? (Shaibu, 2014) This is because even the Asian population is feeding fat under the wealth, there were able to negotiate for their vast population through their continued shift of demands to trade with the African continents. This helps us to realize the potential of the African continents as those powerful enough not to be not overlooked nor portray as those relegated as powerless continents. Even so, how should Africans themselves resolve to lead their continent without believing in different interest, navigating their existence under foreign controls? At the same time, Most Chinese intellectuals wrote off democratic ideology of which this thinking continues to date. E.g., Yu Keping of Beijing University argues that democracy makes simple things "overly complicated and frivolous" and allows, "certain sweet-talking politicians mislead the people." Thus, why should not Africa strikes a balance steps to re-direct the course of their own history into a relatively enduring path to their posterity liberty, safety, peace, stability, sense of purpose? The era of African instability, lack of integration and changing the map of Africa the way we know it today is fast attracting a perfect date with history. Although, African leader hardly recognized it but the 21st century will surely subdue this historical deposit course on the African continents through the Western tact towards Africa (Shaibu, 14th March 2014)

Stages 7

African Postcolonial Development Authenticities:
How easy?

The Only African Hope That Could Bring Stability; and
Sustainability Throughout The Continent

Feasibly, the roots of African poverty, uncertainties, un-development, violent and the current states of affairs, terrorism could merely be settled only when the African leaders decided to confront the continent challenges within their nation states. To face these pots of evil situations in the Africa continent may demand us to inquire. How African could realize their own potentials in the world politics? How neither could African nations be established, nor should it be reconstruct to simultaneously answer the demands of its destiny and people? As many of us already know about the African continent, the nations called democratic today in Africa were all gathered under a pretense of false amalgamation and creation which does not in any dimension reflects how a nation state could or should be established in any parts of the civilized world. Nevertheless, the West demands that Africans countries must be democratized. To whose benefit does democracy in Africans states applied? The whole nations in Africa were cut like a piece of cake signifying high levels of interest by the powerful individual nations of the past centuries during the dark ages as mentioned somewhere in this text. This state of affairs had continued to hunt many African continents into decays by wars, violence, mistrust, terrorism, etc. making even Africans to understand each other as enemies instead of brothers.

Insightfully, we must realized that the states of anarchy in today's Africa continent from a realistic point of view were never an African making but the for the interest of the elsewhere colonizers who set the light of wars and violence, hatred and mistrust were constructed into the African people's mine which conventionally and collectively calculated under the language differences in Africa by the West to achieve one common objectives of dominating and continue to keep demoting the African people through their various African leaders collaborator. Therefore, for African to first cultivate any kind of culture to arrest their disorganized societies, the roots of their political beliefs in the existence institutions must be challenged. This view in African had been left a decade without questions and as such, every political leader in African had to constantly hold onto the preserved civilizations as the only ways to grasp their nations together without waking up to see the hammering damaging the preserve fabricated nations had cost their integration and peaceful existent. For example, a country like Slovenia with a population of only around 2 million, according to the 2012 estimate had secure a right to be independent with a mere five ethnic groups with where the highest ethnic were Slovenes by a ratio of 83.1%. Therefore, why should Africa population with vastly different identities for generations which had nothing in common as one nation be positioned as non-negotiable to separate irrespective of war and violence over the false state-hold their exhibits as nations in Africa? Thus, the transformation of imperial powers in the aftermath of most Africans independence in the 60s through a change of colours as leaders does not change its original design exploitations, but rather it re-produces an indistinguishable suitcase with a merely little to secure for Africa stability from exploitations of the so called representative leaders. African must agree that the lands under their control today is the major set-back to their development and progress and this is because there does not represent the interest of the people of Africa wither their ever increasing population in the continent as equal citizens with equal liberty in the states of nations in Africa as sovereign states today.

For examples, some of the biggest challenges in Africa today is not only about their population growth, poverty, uncertainty, corruption etc. However, the biggest Africans problems is that; who is actually a rightful citizen in the various states of sovereignty Africans today occupied at post-colonialism? Politically, when we look from various historical contexts and dimension, asking the real questions as under which root-dragon design did African's instability, uncertainties have been gained over the years as many groups of African societies today and their leaders have ideologically channeled forcefully to marginalize the minorities under their charge for a buoyant gift? Which is a term regularly called protecting the pre-colonial existing states as nations manufacture by God? In addition, not to be tempered with as to give autonomous for groups to find their own democratic destiny. It is believes of this book that Africa continent had been perverted from its history but have not stopped the continent from realizing their very original destiny. Until such recognition are being carefully assembled by the Africans to see themselves as same people, but distinguish by the imperialism inclination according to their own aims in Africa and destiny to fabricate a falsehood democratic status for them, these manipulated ideas cultivated into the continent is only necessary to keep the leftover imperial laws while in another tunnel to maintain fine-turning African existent under the Western control. Although, as we know already, this view hardly permit Africans to be free realize their own liberty and sovereignty since independence. Is there any thought to say neither knowing that an occasion will come when the Western view of Africans will be disappearing soon? Even with the contemporary present of Chinese's evolution into the African continents. Unless the African people decide to challenge their fear with courage and purpose, hardly will anything tangible will change in Africa throughout the cause of any form of human era on earth. As I look into the future of Africa, the shift will be strong, enough and further being capable of assimilating African people with one another, so that integration with one another with one common shared purpose to survive beyond poverty level, inequality within the nations both within and regionally, etc. would be achieved. Occasionally, this challenge often piloted the majority of African peoples into disunity. A ilk of fiction and further possible potent driving many African countries into a severe war, violence, wars and terrorism in the 21st century. Nevertheless, If Africa must survive, the footing of what tight them together as one country must be loose by the African as one of the most significant traps setting the countries into wars and violence from Congo to Nigeria, South Africa between the strangers and original owner of the land, Mali, etc.

Stage 8

The prolongation of EX- in the African Continent;

Causes of Africans Political Crashes, Anarchy, Terrorism
'Throughout the Continent of Africa'

The state of wars and violence had suddenly become the modern African trademarks; However, African's elite never expected this situation initially but the imperial architects of colonialism are fully aware of the bottle states of violence and instability being devised into the Africans continent. Especially at the close of imperial un-ceremonial, exist from the continent of Africa. On the other hand, the questions remain under what situation does the constant African states of wars, instability, violence and terror of terrorism emanated? On the contrary, today, many Africans states have been made disabled to see themselves as powerless of securing stability for their people and generation yet unborn. While at the time when many countries all over the world, are generating peaceful integration towards one common existence, many of the African continents and their countries are living under a pretext of transforming their different countries by wetting their personal wallet abroad and also building a castle on earth. Consequently, this delightful mix of hope for the people in poverty and in another dimension concern for self-aggrandizement had to project Africa continent as the worst continent around the world to deliver from their deceptions. This is even when it was open to the entire world that African challenges are primarily under the shadow of self-produced by the African people and because of such, a continuation with imperial tent without a vision for the African youths posterity. It significantly means Africans leaders are so pitiless to their own land and disrespectful to their historical unique values. Ideally, this situation often happens only many African leaders climbed into a position of being another black imperialist. The whole continent of Africa had to be group into various sources of violence and wars looking from each African country in Africa since independence as the highest value the fabricated nation states could exhibits. For example, a country in Africa like, Liberia, Congo, Sudan, Mali, Senegal is referred are 'war zones while Nigeria, North Africa, Niger is most likely referred as a terrorist haven. So, regardless of what many African countries maybe have been designated nor called by their formal colonizers in both past and present, the true situation of whatsoever challenges African continent faced today are the vision and projects of the imperialist. Furthermore, the present of today's African leader's creation of high-level inequality carefully design to help the West to secure themselves the needed foreign policies of their continent from the Africa society's resources. This sentiment was also echoed by Mandela in the early in 1955 during the black struggle against the white minority rule over their country when he said the requirements for a free and democratic country, anticipated that 'changes envisioned would never be achieved without a radical vision to altering the economic and political structure of the southern African nation states. Thus, despite the African long struggles against disunity, colonialism, despotic and the militarization of the entire democratic country's state in Africa, the questions are very much demanding if the African leaders actually envision any kind of mental picture to altering the ruthlessness of inequality, politics of aggrandizement, deceptions and calculated the ratio of poverty on the continent? Even though that African leader's continued to misjudge their ineptitude in administering their individual states due to lack of mission and understanding the impacts it continues inflects in their societies in general, the twenty-first century had to adequately bring along its dexterous waves under which African must changes else, African unity, integration, development will hardly ever be sustained. This is because many African countries had failed to demand justices' in the continent through a negotiation that could maintain an ever-lasted integration of purpose to their existing half-baked states as democratic nations. Even so, as the case may likely be not, the future on the continent seems essentially nor partly partition along a long-distance mission to anarchy instead of integration. Also, there is a non-conformity of many leaders in Africa to declare jointly desires to re-shape the states to meet globalization demands, except a simple command for unity through a kind of compact negotiation between themselves, also widely illegitimate political vote rigging by a piloted political nugget called 'supports' had to continue to immorally display African people lack of understanding about the essentiality of a democratic movement nor transitions. As we could see in most African countries today, how to negotiate a peaceful resolution about how to reject the past creations of states in Africa and as well to reduce the victims of imperial design marginalization of the whole regions into the single state are one central ideology damaging the statues of unity in Africa continent. Particularly, on the questions of how should Africans take charge of their continent, people and resources to the benefits of their valuable existence is one basic and key problem African faced as challenges. Indeed, there is a kind of 'set up" found by the diminishing imperial powers that conquered African state to continue with their formal elsewhere ideas of imperialism in Africa. We can see this view from numerous trade agreements with the West, Asian partly and even Indian soft-power politics and diplomacy in Africa. African is seen by major diminishing super influential powers as the key economic hub for their country's interests and sustainability. Above that, nothing more is important about Africa in the faces of the Western countries. An idea many African states are not aware nor often play self-politics of sampling their people's liberty, freedom and rights for their aggrandizement. Perhaps, Africans believe that the coming of the Europeans into their continents, and its implication does not depart with the West at the post un-prepared loose from Africa in the 50s down to the 80s. Nevertheless, what virtually changed in Africa since the aftermath of decolonization in the 60s? Thoughtfully, it is my belief that only the Africans history can truly judge its leaders since independence in the 60s. For instance, the West, who visionary brought Christian religions to the African continent, does not in any measures advanced in Christianity as black Africans in almost the entire world today. What is wrong with Africans as people who never seems to learn from their history? The question at present is whether the Europeans do believe in God from the real sense of the God? Take for instance, 'To protect democracy, African must adapt to the Western ideology of the human right as the West indicates in their political diplomacy towards Africa. In fact, who actually give the West the right over the African people and the continent? Democracy nor its deception's ideology is not what will sustain African states from its an advance insufficient in human and resource development, but an ability of the West to regard Africans as equal partners and as human by entering into an identical trade deal, developments with realistic measures without any hidden agenda will set the decaying African states on the right way to build up. This view implies that, any negotiation for the development of African people should engage directly with the African population instead of the continue of imperialistic policy of 1884-1885 where the act of Berlin conference was initiated, prepared and stamped without African people but were invented for the interest of those who could benefit from the African resource. We may even ask ourselves today, who does the cake sharing of African benefit today? In the case of injustices, African people are very much living with an endless and excruciating devastation cause to the continent by the Western world in both past during the slavery, colonialism, post-colonialism and the neo-colonial-imperial idea's plot in a new suitcase into African state in both past and present. Perhaps, as such that these demonic situations continue, African challenges for survive will continue to drive the African people into disunity and wars. However, the sincerest question on the slate of African leaders today is to ask whether there has truthfully envisioned one idea for the African people beyond what they are elsewhere formal colonizers choose for them? Why African leaders should be walking in the fear of the Western leaders who does not believe in their continent integration, unity, growth, liberty beyond their own need for the African wealth? The opinion expressed in these books is that of sympathy for the African generation yet unborn as their future look may not look blinks nor even as bitter as worse given the current plotted collaboration damaging African integrations and unity. As the current inevitable challenges facing the countries in Africa are getting beyond the control of neither the continent owns representatives, who are vitally representing themselves instead of the people's interest. This is because each dispensation nor regimes since independence in Africa seem to work to advance the connected inspirations for decades as the historical data vertically indicated. Nevertheless, I will suggest that the way forward for nearly everyone African state is to recognize the mess currently existing in their continent and further device a distinguish policies needed in order to elevate its people and their societies. This view signifies that All Africans must come into a compact integration as a key symbol of strategy through dialogue, compromise among themselves with a believes that, most of the preserved states as countries today are surviving under a time-bomb which has to continue to disapprove their development and vast navigation into violence and wars. Until such a demanded radical U- twist is directed to breaking the African continent existing disparity state as countries, no amount of reforms, laws, and the commission could secure the continent peace except a dialogue among countries in Africa to end every imperial created state in Africa. Note; I bear no reflection on the activities of the contemporary African Union (AU), Ecowas, Nepad and other sort of commission established in Africa, which could not initiate any considerable policy to cross ban imperial state created in Africa. This is why every effort to initiate democratic principles in Africa would not merit progress, but rather delving tall into anarchy, insecurity, violence. And no measures adequately design to collectively respond to various crises in the majority of African's state by their leaders. This is because in most cases, African's citizens are being dehumanized but only to be highlighted as *'Rebels'* and get them murdered. It is extremely disturbing to see how African's citizens are being killed by Africans and further have been labeling them as 'Rebels.'. It is only in Africa that one could repeatedly see a peaceable citizen fighting over injustices and for their rights being labeled as 'Rebels.'. While in most so calls, democratic countries recognize most sometimes their citizen's demand by a peaceful dissolution of government. In Africa style of democracies, any attempt to logged rioting will amount to millions been put to death by their government. It is so irritating. Even so, African's hardly learn lessons that could lead them into salvation. In my individual observation, the ideal shift by African to face African questions one after the other, especially those of violent, wars, anarchist societies and the constant instability, poverty, terrorism radicalisms, sticking inequality established and preserved by African's elites is to permit a free flow of moral conscience into the vein of most African leaders so that there could be able to compare their societies with those of their foreign collaborator who help them to defraud their own societies to develop their people. This may sound as key music to echo into many generations of African youth if Africa state must survive. Morally, in the real sense of sympathy, it occurs to me that Africans elites must cultivate a moral conscience into securing African people liberty, integrity and equality so that, they could glimpse. How delightful is the poverty ratio behind their so called wealth without a strong unity, integration within their continent and as such a solid foundation could be initiated by Africans, build viable institutions for their people so that states in Africa could be secure as lasting institutions for the unborn African posterity.

Stage 9

The Shaking Walls in the African Continent:
Which Ways Seem Active For The Africans Liberation?

"Africans Youth demands the truth concerning

the foundation of their continent failures. Even so, this shortcoming were not invented during my birth but I have acquire a knowledge around the radical situation of Africans societies that could help provide Africa youths with a viable realities to their questions from the continent historical mess untold about Africa exploitations" (Shaibu-April 2014)

It has remained a quite long-lasting enigma in Africa continent about the true situation of their failures throughout the last decade. Nevertheless, the truth that could emanate to lighten the continent concurrent causes of political instability in the region of African state remain in a caged despite post-colonialism. But it is not to all conclude that such violent revolutions are the making of African people and respective societies. On the other hand, most countries across the world today face several challenges in different perspectives and dimension. In these domains, I decide to focus on the evolution of African causes of instability by trying to hold a comparative look at how other country's institutions are being created nor even manufacturers over the past decade between fifteenth centuries to the contemporary 21st century. This test may yield us a kind of positive result, which helps us to account for the decaying infrastructures calls states in Africa continents. Thus, one of these supreme questions in the African continent is the dilemma of countries being stagnated at the lowest human standard and how this situation could be over-turn or even to unlock how the vision of the Europeans historian tradition engagement into Africa should be assumed. Until then, it is roughly difficult to neither actually understand nor at most reject the Western interest and perceptions in relation to the African people. This is at the back of the Western world simultaneously continues to deny African realities as an essential partner by focusing exclusively on the problems of the continents as a strategic policy in securing their home states from Africa a well-needed resources for their national interest and development as well as leading us to essential questions about the shaking institutions in Africa continents.

Stage 10

Re-examining European Navigation Into A Stable Integration, Democratization & Union:

What Lessons For African Youths?

At the outset, when decide we look at European state creation after the Second World War. This is one of the periods in the faces of the majority of Europeans who will never be forgotten quickly. A period marked by economic reconstruction, political instability and at the beginning of the cold war. The European searching for a mechanization to secure them a free liberty to collective integration, putting ends to wars, forging unity among themselves, had too stretches their arms towards a system to be known today as 'widening integration' by the Paris treaties in 1951 establishing the European Coal and Steel Community with the lasting validity of 50 years which However, by 1952, which was the view of the original (5) countries. France, Germany, Italy and Benelux and Netherland. How as time passes, in 1973 United Kingdom, Northern Ireland and Demark to join the groups of four, which today reflecting how the maps of European Union were both established and at the same token changes how the European wider integrations for the general market policy were all found. Until 1981 when the Greece joins the Union and Portugal and Spain entry in 1986, the European community keeps asking questions about how to end wars and to build a constructive future for their young generation both born and unborn. Furthermore, In the middle of 1990s seeing the operation of the compact integrations between the groups in the Union, East Germany joins in 1990s, to follow suit by Austria in 1995 with Sweden and Finland and further to strengthening their economic thought, and political integration and for a strategic Deeping ideology, Cyprus, Malta co-join in 1994 with Bulgaria and Romania in 2007. So, to cut a long story short, the underlying ideologies of the completely unique and compact European policy Union today were as a result of the French ideologist Foreign Minister Robert Schuman given his unforgettable speech in early 5th May 1950s. One of the dates in itself as European celebrating the date. A date known fully as remarkable to observe consistently by the entire Europeans countries for sharing possessions between themselves as well as rendering political, social, policy and strategy development among their part. We could immediately see how the compacts of European integrations were initiated and further established with a mandate to ensure efficiency and among other things, liberties and freedoms of their citizenry through integration of the Europeans Union. An astonishing record of envisioning closeness among each other as well as creating an equal opportunity to their fellow members in solving their several economic problems after the wars and its destruction, resolving differences among nations of fellow members in the Union through monetary terms, making a fresh map for the Europeans to forging a new political road map and political dimension, which could foster growth and developments among the member nations respectively. Furthermore, see, Ralph Folsom[4] further clarifications of the history of the European Union. It may equally important will conceivably be true to say that the ideological ground for the creation of the European Union may have existed before the treaties of Paris in the 1951. For examples, Victor Hugo wrote in 1849"A day will arrive, where all countries of this continent, without giving up their particularities or their well-known individuality, will come together closer to a higher community and lay the foundations of the big European brotherhood. A day will arrive where there will be no other battlefields than the markets, which opens for trade, and the spirit which opens the ideas. A day

---

[4]   Ralph Folsom, the European Union; Part One, July 25 2012. University of San Diego School of Law

will arrive bullets, and bombs will be replaced by ballot papers[5]" which we have all witness to continue stimulations and consistency, rejecting any sorts of wars while the Europeans keep drawing upon their past historical evolution to break out of wars with each country within the European background respectively. How can we visualize the AU establishment and its uses as a visionary institution in the African continent? At first, we must recognize from the historical evidence that the African past. See Basil Davidson in the African past[6] it was documented by the past Western historians who African people were not thought to have entered into the grand circuit of the world development. Having no history of their own, they were manifest 'children who had *failed to grow up*'. See Basil, Pp.22. Thus, given that even international laws are being regarded as 'serviceable instruments.' What can we say about the African problems since post-colonialism and the AU vision and policy towards African people, unity, integration, common trade, loose zone, currency? Etc., the act which founds the AU on July 11th, 2000, a creation out of the default organization of African Unity (OAU) could as matter of fact had been stagnated from its design and missions to fostering African stability, cooperation, economic constructive stability, science and notwithstanding the revolutionary distribution of unrestrained entry

---

5   See, the 1925 the French Minister of Foreign Affairs, **Aristide Briand**, said at the occasion of the Locarno Pact (Locarno is a little town on the Italian sea, where a peace pact has been signed): "In Locarno we spoke European, this is a new language, which has now to be learned".

6   Basil Davidson, the African past, chronicles from Antiquity to the modern times. PENGIUM LIBRARY. 1966, PP 17-33.

to various African regions. Perhaps, what is utterly incomprehensible to many of us intellectual thinker of African origin like me is to understand how African states keep a history of degenerative, underdevelopment, sentimentalism and poverty within the empires held tight to hold without any visible agenda for a progressive shift of tactics and policies, which could elevate African people and continent beyond dependency despite a massive political propaganda of the African leaders? "We are trying" after all, Rome was not built in a day. This explanation may have also appeared accurate to the next stops on the AUs policies and tactics over the years. The AU had spelt out conditions that hold, in reality, failed to challenge the difficulties the African people faces in the continent of black people beyond the basic problems of already known effects of common integrations and as such, African leaders' skillful views and policy hardly to remember African's pains, fighting to realize them nor yet they carry out attempts that could one day aspire to be achieved. For examples, The AU Act establishes a requirement as "the necessary conditions which will enable the continent to play its rightful role in the global economy and international negotiations[7]." Forgetting that the obvious key problem's of the African continents first is to

---

[7]   See, Conflict of interest in Africa; A. Bolaji Akinyemi, The Organization of African Unity and the Concept of Non-Interference in Internal Affairs of Member-States, 46 Brit. Y.B. Int'l L. 393 (1972-73) (discussing how the effectiveness of the OAU could be improved if the OAU stops hiding behind the non-interference clause of Article III (2)); Obi Okongwu, The OAU Charter and the Principles of Domestic Jurisdiction in Intra-African Affairs, 13 Indian J. Int'l L. 589 (1973).

recognize themselves as one people. II, Article 3 spells out the purposes of the AU, which conditionally including a move towards achievement of "a greater unity and solidarity between the African countries and the peoples of Africa. With my convincing memory, The African leaders themselves do not believe in themselves, but rather sees AU as a place for keeping playing their political sticks called diplomacy. I will argue that for African leaders to succeed in saving African continents, there must initiate a tactical diplomacy to understand their selves first, their continents and their peoples demand irrespective of which regions they came from as Africans. Thus, without such a shift in ideological enterprises in Africa, the visions of African people will always continue to be in shambles. It does not matter to see the political calculation in the AU Acts which specifies on the acceleration of "the political and socioeconomic integration of the continent. Also, as this view sounds convincing, how many Africans can travel freely within the African states? As it is in most European continents? Are African leaders failing their people or walking under a pretext of 'capitalist individualism'? The AU thought about the ideology for the 'Promotion of "peace, security, and stability on the continent" had always lived until death without a proving mandate of reality as tools for solving African imbalance since decolonization. We may also be interested to know that the AU Article (4) contains the principles upon which the Union will function, such as "sovereign equality and interdependence among Member States of the Union' some of which still remains neither inadequate nor even neglected in acting for the general interest of the African masses. The AU Act, which also enshrines the sanctity of colonial boundaries, 'uti possidetius juries see had to also suspend the issues of sovereignty in Africa, especially those politically, economically, ethnically marginalized by the Western Europeans intrude to the African metropolis. It has politely been argued that uti possidentis was intended to serve both an external and internal purpose; "superficially, it would try to prevent irredentist tendencies by neighbors from turning into territorial claims and the potential role of force. Internally, it would give clear notice to ethnic minorities that secession or adjustment of borders was not an alternative." The genuineness in the 21st African states is to see how such decaying policies had project Africans into most violent wars. On the other hand, the questions on how to patch up uti possidetis with a development mission of the AU in African continent without tempering the existing 'map' is one fundamental diabolism in Africa. Whose ultimate intention does the law on retaining the imperial artificial boundaries actually served? This has been one of the defective thoughts of African leaders by holding intangible' fruits as something to be conserved for the generations.'. Without a switch or a radical removal of the imperial crafted map in African by the African people relocating to their initial origins, how can any move towards democratic development be achieved on the continent of Africa for a more unique integrated of their disorganized identity? Undoubtedly, Could this situation take us back to the Western view of the African people are like kids who lack a history of their own, nor even try to convince the world they had one shared history, which is commonly known as black? Perhaps, many problems which I would like to emphasis on the issues which surround Africans, and the AU is about how Africans themselves sees each other as black people. For instance, walking on the street of the Czech Republic, a formal huge communist economic empire, one could see many black people who may prefer to declare their origin from a different continent of the world without an effort to remember they are blacks. This African peoples I try to engage in an attempt to draw out a sketch of this book failed to even talk to me about their original home, nor even choose to defend their country of residence as their creative home. Nowadays, several of them lose contact with the African reality as it appears to me, many of them decided not to see Africa as the continent that could escape its misery at some days on earth. Does not this think sound irritated? It also comes to my mind that many of them might not understand the core Europeans histories, terrors of the first world wars, second world wars and the existing never-ending cold war's within the so call super powers. Thus, to fast track the African music, Africans do not believe in their country, continent and historical development, which serve to damage their own history while putting it back with the perpetually amassed African failures to pursue their realities as people with a history. We May even agree that the AU inability nor ineffectiveness does not the parade it from the African leaders alone, but most Africans failed themselves because there do not see their self as ever capable of changing their own home, continents and history? The questions now in Africa are: how can African retrace their history for a sustainable development, integrity, integration and stability if there do not believe in their collective individual institutions? See Shaibu, 2013) who is against the Nigeria democracy? Many Africans cannot travel within African freely since the development of African strategic cooperation calls Ecowas, OAU. And now AU. Without any significant tribute to a peaceful resolution for sighting the African place in the human history. One of the most reasons why much of severe havoc is being caused in the African continent by every race of the world is simply that, the African person's attitude to each other as coming from one genetic race. For examples, traveling to Uganda, South Africa, Nigeria, Sudan, Ethiopia, Cameroon as African, one needs visas, nor where is no visa, one faces brutal treatments at the border of most African countries. Why should African not recognize the needs to admit themselves as one people? I often see the problem of African people is most primarily stations at morality, common sense; sentiments attributed mainly to the imperial subjugation of the African continents in the early fortieth century, which have radically broken the African cultures, traditions with each other as citizens of one continent. This situation had to significantly contribute to the contemporary collapse of African sentiment for not believing in themselves as originating from one single black coil and this impact has virtually continued to be leading Africans into decays as dubious states and character had been preserved. This interaction may even lead to the recent questions on how the African leaders since 2003 Burundi accord on peace keeping in Darfur in 2007 and the issues that surrounding the security council in the UN as some significant countries in Africa, e.g. South Africa and Nigeria, Algeria often tracks down by non-compliance with one collective ideology towards one another in mechanizing a central initiation that could help them to achieve one common objectives but rather chooses to jealously watch each other arrogantly on who should control the African hegemony, see also [8](Shaibu, 2012) African Hegemony; who is in command of Africa? The reasons for the African continent's failure to make a realistic policy decision for the continent and countries are questions linked to the above-mentioned items. However, others are; (a) African nations must be ready in taking a step to establish a policy towards unifying the whole African continent as people of different accent, but belonging to one shared groups as 'black origins.' There must see them in any part of the world as one are in the struggle for one collective goal, which is unity, Integration, stability and for the development of the people souls decaying in wars and poverty created nor invented by their history and today in collaborated by

---

8

Shaibu, On African foreign Policy. Editor by Martin Riegl, Jakub Landowsky) Strategic and Geopolitical Issues in the Contemporary World Hardcover – July 1, 2013

their own people to defraud their continent's rights and liberty, (b) For the AU, there is no trick that could secure them stability of purpose without first to secure for themselves one universal determination and believe to elevate their regions, continent, people by taking one central and visionary position with a collective plan to fighting an African cause. Therefore, in as much as the AU continues to be played by domestic and influential political tricky among African leaders, the African vision of stability from wars, poverty, underdevelopment, the dependency will consistently lead African nations into instability and lawlessness. (c) African people must accept their citizens as one person irrespective of the countries there were born, but as far as there are black people, there should try to envision collective desires to foster developments among themselves so that peace and unity should prevail in the continents being regarded as jungles for acquiring wealth. Although, it is my opinion that one day, the African continent will forcefully recognize a cause to foster unite among themselves (Shaibu, 2014, in Prague Brno). This view I fell shall elevate the continent beyond even disappearance one day by wars to be caused by the alarming poverty, terrorism and political deception. This word will enhance and greatly begun to afford our people's liberty to pursue their ambitions within the African continent without focusing on moving to the Western Europe for their survival. We must develop our own civilization if African must be sustained in unity. Where we can improve our particular ideas, we have to initiate a policy which may begin from here; the black people of Africa hereby agree to initiate this compact policy to elevate our people strengths in their own continent, etc. so that African people could be freely developed into one unique society of black democracies of the world. (Shaibu, 2013). This I offer to the African generation born and the unborn posterity to be a nagging testimony of the African losses and disunity. As recorded in the history of European integration policy, Jean Monnet remembered in his memoirs the spirit of this conference: "We are here to undertake a general task – not to negotiate for our own national advantage, but to seek it to the advantage of all. Only if we pursue to eliminate our historical deficiency could our realities achieve. Undoubtedly, Debates without any particularistic feelings between each region of Africa shall we reach Africans a solution. In so far as we, gathered here, can change our methods, the approach of all Europeans will, likewise, gradually change ."". Conclusively, what should be the African national pride is not their abundant resources, *but should be the centre on ldentifying themselves first as African black people*? This discovery could at a distance future set Africans on a part of salvation. It does not matter how long it may take for the majority of Africans to read this book by the real Africans of desires to solving the stagnating Africans splits, but it will surely help Africans to realize themselves as people of a continent with wealth abundantly in sufficient degree to set the entire world's food supply. So, African's continents are not poor, neither you ask yourself, which country around the world could boast of what African stored in their backyards? *It is a matter of time; Africans will deliver their continent, even without word transitions to democracy*. One must point at his front to choose the directions of next steps ahead of them. African recognizes you as a continent with equal opportunity to lead the world. It does mean, recognizing where one stands at particular moments and the time of such decisions. This ends the blemishing of the African societies as known integrated and sound intellectual making in the human history (Shaibu, 2013).

Stage 11:

The African Instability, Democracy and Sustainability;

"The Changing Phrases in the African Politics"

A political order emerges because of the achievement of some equilibrium between the contending forces within the society. Even so, as times go on, changes occur internally and externally, which may further face new terms of political integration nor trade, or imported ideas as a result, the preceding equilibrium no longer holds, and political decay's results until the existing actors come up with an up-to-date set of rules and institutions to restore the order. See Francis Fukuyama on the root of political order. Surely, to drive deeply into the present time parliamentary turmoil's in the African continent, We may likely be baffled to see that the post colonial--existing African customary identity as 'fragile states,' which has been a framed disability to entire African people by the Western counterpart has today totally been ignored and further postponed even at the cost of Africans dilemma. Not just that, some key issues of business organization to many African regions in the present time as 'identify with dependency' had in the past drags Africans into a shocking stress by a cluster of jointly confusion design before the African independence in the 60s. This occurred by the imperial strangers from West into Africa nevertheless. Most of their various policies are irregular assumed about the uniqueness of African people and to value the continent cultures. However, what the Western world recognizes at this period was only how to turn states in African into a kind of semi-Western tool. Whose must follow all European shared liberal beliefs, ideology, traditional and organized lifestyle of the West as it was initiated in 1914 to eliminate African realities? Until this, unjust predictor states of mind by the West in Africa continent are totally broken down, it will hard for African states to release themselves from the chain of the Western hug to progress. Although, These shares artificial tactics by the Western Europeans had to charge most of the African continent and their people into a state of confusion despite independence in the 60s. Africans indeed lost their significant sense of reasons and by doing things in their traditional capacity. Who is to blame by African predicaments today? This loss of enriching cultural share's values had consequences on which the contemporary institutional disruptions had found its spaces in the existing political structure's exhibits by the majority of the Africans leaders of the nation. At most, this shocking elevation of artificial boundaries, false -fully created the West had to define the ways the African Politics and policies should be activated as prophetic democratic societies without African trying to inquire into how efficiently to kick off a new question into evaluations of thoughts on how to machining African people a brand of antivirus up-to-the-minute vision to eliminate these threats of decaying political profile the continents of Africa preserved today. Nevertheless, this is especially on the issues on how the Europeans co-jointly demarcate the continents of Africa into a portion of the meal forming unusual institutions for Africans who in the context of political state creation does, not in authenticity. In the same way, this situation had to considerably attribute procedures as close up links to the African people inspiration for human elevation beyond poverty echelon as the case indicates the contemporary Africa continent. Thus, understanding that African cultural and institutional realities had been disband from the early 1914 were over 99 % of the African policies, structures, common language, customs had been changed without African reversing to demanding their political rights to reforming the current status of donated states, how could African initiate a convincing policy towards a democratization which demanded a uniformities by collective purpose, consideration to common equality before the laws nor facing the challenges of the existing vast different languages in the continent of African states?

Nevertheless, the existence of purely African cultural and traditional values could increase the chances of democratic norms if it can still exist today, especially if we count from the aspect of key rational traditional values of each African society before the imperial subjugation. Obviously, One of the undoubtedly truth this book could argue is that the Africans were not as matter of ever increasing Western strategic policy towards African to empower the continent's development beyond dependency and as such, the sad truth should be noticed as the African people has been viewed as not capable of initiating staging a radical policy in their continent which could demand Europeans changing their own ways seeing African people and their respective government tangible global compact. This list of political and strategic calculation the African had to effectively undermine their superiority in the global market given the African outstanding natural resource wealth. For instance, who initiate how resources are being traded in the public market? The buyer to the owner of the product? It is the owner who owns the products should determine how much he or she contributes to the production of such commodities. Ideally, as we could understand nor see from all round the world geopolitical calculations. The Europeans who do not logically have the solid minerals nor the goods often set down in neither London, Germany nor even US to determine how African resources should be sold. How did the West Arrived at a convincing reality that such movements will remain forever without questioning? Let's not forget that it is the way the West see the other emerging power in both Africa, Asians and the closing link to the Russians that is causing the world unsafe for the majority of the whole world citizens through violence, wars, terrorism and even through a political trick which may leads to another 3rd world wars in Africa. For instance, we saw Iraq politically framed into anarchy and institutional instability, Afghanistan, Egypt's, Libya, Syria and the current issues in Iran are totally tied to the wars of interest instead of those preparing countries for democratic movements where human liberty should be guaranteed and protected. Likely, the wars in African states especially on the battle field between Nigeria and Cameroon on the nagging questions of Bakassi people of Calabar Nigeria which there were transferred un-ceremoniously to Cameroonians had leads to million put to death at almost every instances since the post-colonialism despite the UN intervention and subsequent negotiation until around 2002 where Nigeria decided to hand over

[9] Shaibu, 2012) The Memory of Berlin Conference 1884-1885; African Questions "What matters in the 21st century? A paper presented at the international conference of Young scholars. Also, see **M. Mbuh**. (2004) International Law and Conflicts: Resolving Border and Sovereignty Disputes in Africa. I Universe, Inc.460 pages, Lord Salisbury, in "Bakassi who has Bakassi?" (West Africa 18-24 April 1994) (ISBN: 0595297072

their own language people, lands to the Cameroonian government on the judgment many legal luminaries, diplomats and scholars a political fraud to the Nigerian by the West government. See, [9](Shai bu, 2012, perhaps, in the case of African geopolitics, the West political calculation is to exploit the African resources without commiserating the continents with any visible like the hold of transforming the continent into a better society of human elevation beyond poverty level. For examples, the British spent almost 60th years in Kenya in exploiting the country without a railway to positioning the country easy access to quick transportation and not does this ends there, education, state society structures, etc. As it was the same in Tanzania etc. all were demolished to beggary institutions such as the current Congo situation stand today. No single IDEAS seem real by international laws to ending the wars in Congo and neither the presence of the United nation since the 1960s with Congo help in accelerating peace re-union of the disorganized states by the Belgium King Leopold who single handedly own a country bigger than his own original country Belgium. As I remark in the closing part of my presentation on the question of the memory of the Berlin conference in 1884-1885, I categorically elucidate that 'Where there is no honesty, the memory is lost, where there is no trust, the people are caged. However, we now live in an open world where the waves of colonialism through slave trading will never be existed again. Then, why are we darned much separated by ideology through discriminatory policy over human beings like us? The journey could well be stable, admit one another, and the journey will be sustained if 'only' we recognized that 'we all are equal before God' (Shaibu, pp. 12). Insightfully, the attachment of most African continent into a region of a wretchedly continent in the world politics to partner with leads may also connect us to additionally undeniable questions confronting the African nation's instability, political decays, piloted terrorism, etc.... How the situation in African continents does comes to this miserable and modern handicap the African people found themselves under the pretext of 'protecting fragile unity in African continents without endings for the Western crucial exploitative delight into African domestic affairs? Let's not hurriedly forget quickly about the ongoing French government decisive entry into the central African without even the agreement of neither the AU Union nor the UN Security Council on the issues of political violence in the Central African Republic region in Africa. This view may have echoed an extra fresh dimension replicating a kind of dynamism if we also want to speak about the recent occasion were the French government had circulated their strategic troops into the central African republics on the pretext of claiming that the Central African Republic is at the break of wars, which was immediately rejected by the setting president.... When he said recently, "There's no genocide, there is not even an inter-religious war. All of this is made up to manipulate the opinion of the international community[10]," We

---

[10] http://www.presstv.ir/detail/2013/12/02/337855/african-genocide-pretext-for-

must also be clear when speaking about transferring democracy to the entire African continents. To whose benefits were the initiating policies of democracies in African states glory? Aids, human right etc. one brilliant thought come to mind, Eg. The Egyptians people launched a revolution against the pro-Israeli regime in January 2011, which eventually brought an end to the 30-year dictatorship of former President Hosni Mubarak in February 2011.yet, how does it happen? Again, while the democratically elected government rolls into office, the first democratic benefits were to accept loan from the IMF by signing pacts with the Western ideological traps. For instance, when the Egyptian President Mohamed Morsi of late had come under fire from several Egyptian activists for bidding a loan of $4.8 billion from the IMF they say such a loan could make Egyptian people poorer which later lead to the counter revolutions that remove Morsi from power. But, the key problems of Morsi were absolutely hiding from the public secing wishes about the pressure from the West to sign a deal from the IMF which could mean Egyptians continue stagnating under the Western aid repayment. Even so, today Egyptians are now surviving with violence, terrorism, instability, wars due one demand by the West to keep hold on Egyptians homeland. The Egyptian has been experiencing pitiless violence since July 3, when the army ousted Morsi's government, suspended the constitution, and dissolved the parliament and the 'Democracy' in Egypt had undergone another dimension into anarchy. Even

french-plunder/

though that the appointed of Adly Mahmoud Mansour as the new interim president. What future for the Egyptian people living in unity like before could not be ascertained? Thus, in the heart of Egyptian unproductive democratic ideology introduce by the West, the US Secretary of State John Kerry repeatedly arrived in Cairo recently was he met with the Egyptian president on Sunday, saying that he told the Egyptians that US monetary support would depend on Egyptian reforms and the IMF agreement." He continues. It is comprehensible to us that the IMF arrangement needs to be reached, and we need to give the market place some confidence," the US secretary of state said."It is paramount, essential, urgent," Kerry told business leaders[11], "that the Egyptian economy gets stronger, gets to endorse on its feet, and it is very clear that there is a circle of connections in how that can happen. "To attract capital, to bring money back here, to give business the confidence to move forward, there has to be a sense of security, there has to be a sense of political and economic viability." Nevertheless, what is not clear to public is that, the current Egyptian government seems not ready to parade his people into such undemocratic 'Trap Loans' from the world bank the so called 'US' Agent when the Egyptian Deputy Prime Minister Ziad Bahaa el-Din reply, "We have postponed that of (IMF) decision for the time being? We are not under the extreme stress that the previous government found itself in," said

[11]   **Egypt must reach an agreement with IMF, Kerry says;**
    http://www.presstv.ir/detail/2013/03/02/291626/egypt-must-strike-deal-with-imf-kerry/

the deputy prime minister. For instance, of Western knowledge in Africa. The Egyptian under numerous challenges by the pleasure of democratic movement had held sporadic talks with the IMF over a loan possibly worth $4.8 billion to help the country's economy since a 2011 uprising dethroned former dictator Hosni Mubarak. As we have seen, The African continent had been designed by the Western idealist as their spheres of democratic empire for exploitation without giving out any significant transitions with a 'democratic designs drafted to secure the continent galaxies of liberty in their own homeland. In fact, many Egyptian and other Africans cannot even get visas to travel across to the Western countries. This is because they were not given an entry traveling documents and while at home, the country's wealth are being looted, farm land destroyed, economically plotted into sectionalism by different kinds of collaborators for the benefits of the West using the selfish African leaders. All this ideological propaganda in favour 'one principle of democracy' was for the West to stick to power in enslaving the under develop world especially Africans. The Western world is fast running out of strategies to enslave African people and what African people must take into account in order to safe their unborn generations. To get the point right, the emergencies of the Mubarak from power in 2011 may have not been clear to many people and regions within Africa. This is because the Western propaganda seems often to stick permanently in over-shadowing the general public awareness. Yet, the truth story cannot be far distance from knowing in this 21st century.

Thus, globalization had in a real sense of human development uprooted the entire Western plot against the world un-privileged people and as such, the only best strategy I should recommend for the West is for them to realize that those 'dark days are over' by accepting to change towards the direction of the new package of human globalization had brought into our general societies for equal treatment towards one sense of liberty and security. Thus, focusing on any category of industrious leveraged of transparency, accountability, liberty as a benefit of Western democratic ideology to the African people, the sense of equality must take the central stages of democratic liberty as the bases towards our published ideas of liberation. Conclusively, who actually is delivering each other in the real context of human necessities between African and the Western countries? The next chapter opens the discussion on how African people should be perceived as those liberating most westerly democratic empires instead of the erstwhile ageing hegemony in Africa

Stages Twelve

Democratizing Inequality in Africa

The unequal lens; African position in the Western vocabulary
The Euro-centric view that Africa was devoid of state organization and in a legal vacuum during the pre-colonial period is not supported by evidence, and must be eliminated. Similarly, the

argument that the various organized entity's in the African continent was just 'Tribal units' and not sovereign states, must be dismissed. So, it is believed from the African pre-colonial period that the Africans were fully aware of the nature of diplomatic protocol long before the European interceptions with tourist views during the period of their exploitation of the African continent. For instance, as early as sixteen centuries, the illustrious king of the Benin kingdom in the modern Nigeria had sent ambassadors to the Portugal, and the Bornu in the contemporary Northern Nigeria had also sent an Ambassador to the Turkey respectively. While in so many other countries in Africa had neither done that earlier, nor there were left out. For instance, in 1512, the Kongo had an envoy in Portugal and Italy. This could visibly lie ground for the subsequent in discussion that African were not in democratizing position before the Europeans false ideas of introducing the so called 'Civilization' to African's people. It is my contention and suggestions that, We must concur in the 21st century that the whole episodes conducted by the European in African should be recognized only as a reason for exploitations instead of those arguments most Western countries accepted by trying to drive out the blames of the Western aggressiveness of exploiting the continent of Africa by the name of civilization. Mainly, the potent of genocide in the African continent, by which key impact in the African continent remain irretrievable. This position may have escaped from the psyche of most people of the Western countries, especially if critically sketched from the Western scholar position.

Even so, one scholar remains outstanding on his view of African continents as he acknowledges that 'the pre-colonial past is unrecoverable in Africa continent' Davidson Basil[12]. It should be, therefore, assumed that African continent been disorganized through exploitative determination of the West in 1884-1885 Berlin act may have run out strategies after post-colonialism where to shift their blames as the un-making of many African disappearances from their pre-existing historical values and traditions. Nevertheless, we must not forget quickly that the nation state could exist as an entity only if there neither have nor had developed one common set of values, custom, beliefs together inline that their respective ethical values and customs are safe. Where states each one could follow their historical traditions without one imposing its own values on another one as superior. *See,* the cause of Czechoslovakia separation in 1993. On the same token, Przeworski (1991) argue that is the construction of new democratic institutions sufficient to ensure stable democracies? The growth of democracy in the aftermath of the soviet regimes break-down has by many scholars been linked to the institutional disagreement among concern interest. Undoubtedly, realizing from a Przewoski position as European, then under what situation does many European expect many African communities and continent to secure their democratic liberty where they have never agreed nor

---

[12]   See, Jeffery Herbs. (1996-97) responding to state failures in Africa, International security , vol.21,no 3,winter 1996-7.pp.175-183

never collectively negotiate the contemporary sovereignty under which most African states exhibit as independence countries? It should be likely correct and further adequate to agree partially with Jeffery Herbs who suggested to a set of loosening an international practice regarding sovereignty is to allow Africans, finally to have some chances to get their own state structures. I will argue that the neither international community, nor system must recognize that Africans had NO state of their own currency and that those currently existing in Africa, which is collectively the misinterpretation of the African continent by the West, are false and should first be ruled out. This fact, I assume will reassure Africans on the way to their rightful pre-colonial institutions where the values, autonomy and dignity lie. Perhaps, It has been noted by many 'same' Western countries as irreversible. See Basil Davidson, (pp127). But I disagree such assumptions and explanation. There is nothing that is un-reversible on earth. Not even the constitution that bond people together, building constructed by men but only the making of the human being I think is un-reversible. Yet, God that brings had taken away. This should mean it reversible even by God himself reverse man he created by taking him away after being born and calling him immediately. I simply assume that the West have been fooling Africans for a very long time, and African must realize this and radically put an end to those atrocities cause of human kind in African continent living in poverty, violence, unstable countries, boundaries artificially drawn by throwing the same family in a different country. It is these subject of collective lies that had to pencil African continents into confusion and dependency century after even the artificial independence were transferred to the African people. Logically, the principal targets of exploitation of the West had not disappeared nor subsided. Where is the truth and the realization of African states as sovereignty if those sovereignties are not respected? Even while writing this book, the French troops are being loaded in Central African Republic in pursuance of the French grip on the country been polluted by violence and poverty of hunger and difference created by the same colonist ideologist[13]. The African continent has been often regarded as one of the weakest states in the global system see, Jackson on 'Fragile states and the international system, (1996) yet, there did not uncover with clarity how such weakness might have emanated in the African continents. Even the Western liberal thoughts agreed that every legitimate government must have chosen its leaders through some constitutional mechanism on which they broadly agreed[14]. Consequently, we have judged the rest of the Continent we do not know anything about them, false-fully share them like a piece meal, disorganized their historic living as it was for their generation of existence, drive hatred into them through boundaries we created artificially, promoted them with a donated regions

---

[13] France playing dirty game in CAR: S. De Bogou

http://www.presstv.ir/detail/2013/11/30/337501/france-cause-of-colonial-crisis-in-car/

[14] Jackson, (1996) Ibid pp.10

called states which does not conform to any form of state creation in any parts of the world, exploited their wealth and humanity values. Who actually decorate the West as the judge of human liberty, freedom and president without the people's consent? This is because the West have misinterpreted the nature of universal laws that people of the world are different in colours, geographically, linguistically, ethnically, but nothing has changed that make them different as not human, but all same genetics of humanity born to live and dies the same as anything living under the Sun. I will assume that every human being has the rights for their own systems of governance to hold tight to the values of the societies where they found themselves peacefully without anyone ideologically and false-fully disorganizing others on their self-fish interest which had today drafted the whole worlds into chaos of wars and pains. *I am proposing to the African people and the people of my next generation in the African continent to see themselves as one people and in furtherance to this remembrance must accept to deviate from the injustices drafted by the West, nor Asian to hinder their human values, customs, cultures and inspiration but to work together in uplifting their country and differences so that the new African continents could be born (Shaibu,2013).* Which may in all rectifications be different from what currently exist in the continents of Africa? This was my intellectual contribution after I have studied; evaluate the entire African continents from the pre-historical nation holds of Africa to the contemporary African peaceful continent which suddenly turn into war zones that Africans never created. It is in such memories that Ferguson used in the context when he term civil society; he took his position on a debate which had engaged Rousseau in his **Discourse of the Origin of Inequality**—namely when asked the questions "what extent can one say that civilization was advancing rather than declining with the emergence of commercial society[15]" Certainly, it must be quite mistaken or rather to believe that neither the advances made from the eventual decolonization in the early 60s had helped the West to see African continents with an equal lens over the past decade but rather the idea of inequality crafted under the price list, of 'We are assortment of people and superior' had been preserved by many Western countries to see the African people and their wealth as an equal partner for progress and development.. We may also agree that the West has the technologies and the African has the resources under which both are equal to trade together under a considerate term possible without inequality ideology. Yet, the reverse is often taken differently from the Western point of view. As one African soldier Kande Kamara of Guinea origin in Africa who served in the second world wars with French contingent will quote "if we had not fought, if we the black people –had not fought in the Western wars, and been taken overseas, and demonstrated some ability of human dignity, we would not have been regarded as anything[16]".

---

[15]   Murrary Milgate & Shannon C. Stimson (2009) After Adam Smith A century of Transformation in Poliyics and political Economy., Prinston University press oxford.

He tries to lament the African braveness and tactical at the battlefield with a significant achievement in displaying the African potentials beyond the grade the most Western world sees African people while another veteran soldier of African origin observe with clarity" only the French knows what 'we' African did for them. We want them to feel liberated. What greater thing could you do for them? However, Africans had no significant values in the eyes of the West of equal partnership for developing the African resources, but rather prefer to deliberately maintain the exploitation even in the 21st century to the highest level of African been turned down into a war zone because of political collaborators in defrauding Africans by both some African leaders and their deputies. Nevertheless, African realities lie with the significant contribution of this book if African must one day be released into a sustainable integration and stability. I will end this chapter by Quoting Charles Darwin when said;

---

16   Myron Echenberg, (1857-1960) colonial conscripts, pp. 127-145. The Tirailleurs

Senegalais in French. Social history of Africa. Series Editors; Allen Isaacman and Luise

White,

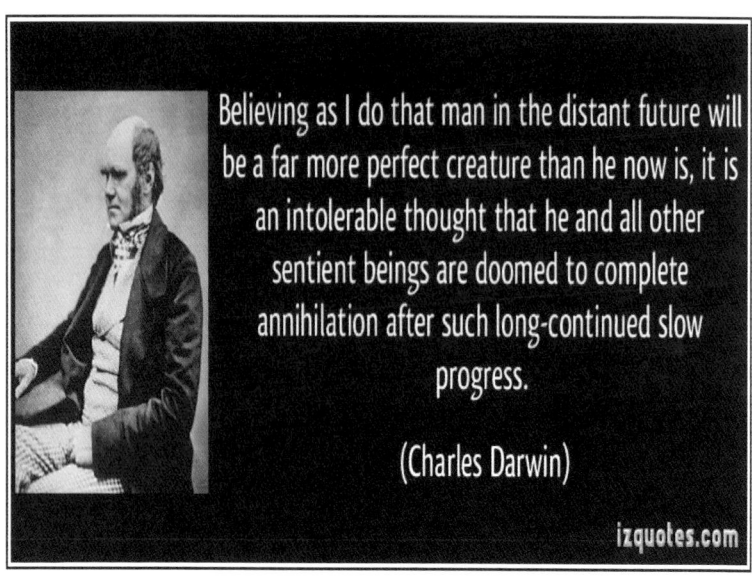

Believing as I do that man in the distant future will be a far more perfect creature than he now is, it is an intolerable thought that he and all other sentient beings are doomed to complete annihilation after such long-continued slow progress.

(Charles Darwin)

izquotes.com

Stages thirteen

Does Democracy Truly Exist in Today's Africa?

Opposing Hybrid Democracy in African States

It is not so long century that we could not locate how democratic state in Africa started. But the concern of this chapter dealt with the issues that surround post-colonialism in today's modern African historic eventual nationhood. But, as the formal secretary general Kofi Anna had been key in emphasizing on designing a road map under which counties in Africans states could be secured and further preserved from its contemporary inadequacies, inequalities, poverty, violence, wars, etc. he had often recognized that "If you have a problem and you cannot find a solution, you will meet again tomorrow and you keep talking until you find a solution. You can disagree with behavior or a particular situation, but you do not resort to calling an opponent worthless". Yet, this burning question demands more than re-designing just as I had mentioned in my previous chapters on African problems. Locating ineffectiveness of must African states are the key questions to the major African challenges not even those Hybrid transformations rocking African states collectively over the past decade of the African design democracy nor artificial states hold as countries. So, without African collective recognition of the movement of their contemporary divide and rule systems, any act of defining simple peace agreements let say between A Hausa community in Nigeria and let's say Igbo communities is not more than what I refer as Hybrid democracies' in Africa continents. As quoted somewhere in Jackson's R. Assessment of Africa so call 'Fragile states," he accepted that one problem of African continents is that they adopted and indeed glorified it, turning it into the basis for a 'nationalism' which was represented as authentically African and which simultaneously re-defined the pre-colonial identifies and political structures as the beginnings of a divisive and illegitimate 'Tribalism'. Furthermore, Bayart (1993-8) acknowledges that one of the key obstacles to African state, especially in the modern states is "The current state system in Africa is a relatively new phenomenon and a foreign import who has been grafted onto existing political and social structures" (Bayart 1993:8). Despite that the compilation of the unfamiliar state creation in the African continents which most Western nations are very much aware it does not look like any form of collective agreement for those countries being assumed as nations. The West still insists that African countries must be democratized as the rest of the Western world. So, given that most African states 'created instead of those from their historical and collective origins, how can African ideas of democracies be defined nor even expected to render a vertical spread of human freedom and autonomy? This is most particularly that most nations are rather donated, never negotiate for collective existence, nor there at some points follow some arrange patterns after post-colonialism. States, for instance, are said to acquire a pre-requisite for legitimacy only where it is constructed, at least in the mind of those who conceived it and minimally actually execute its daily Administrations. Undoubtedly, Buzan claims that in an attempt to get some key answers to two questions on the nature of states contend that; why the states should exist in the form that it does, which may be defined as territorial legitimacy? The second, is why the groups of people who rule it should have any right to act on behalf of those who are merely its subjects or citizens, which may correspondingly be defined as governmental legitimacy[17]? He agreed that such motions are vital to the constitutions of the state's foundation under which states can justify its claims on the people it

[17]   See, Clapham, Christopher S. 1996, Fragile state and international system. African and the international system;the politics of states survival.pp. 1014, African foreign Affairs 1960s

seeks to control. Therefore, considering such a tenthly requirement of state creation procedures, in the case of all African nations, none of such policies were neither forms the views of those who conducted the Berlin acts which had today dismantled the African liberty, freedom, unity and integration nor even let Africans to understand each other as belong to one human race. Other examples are on how most African leaders are being chosen from the post-colonialism. Most Western powers had to stick to the signification of their own involvement in African continents by doing everything dreadful detriments to bring 'who' there wants to power so that there could promote the prosecutions of the Western needed resources from the African continents without considering the implications of the poverty ratio in Africa continents. It has been contested historically that 'for every integration and structural development strategies. It needs to build an environment in which groups feel secure that their identities are not endangered. The greater the disparity in cultural, religious, and racial characteristics, the more complicated the problems. Thus, a multifaceted formula needs here, in which different group's characteristics are looked at positively when comparisons are made. When social comparisons are distinct but equally positive, conflict can be avoided[18]. Consequently, In absolute Western practices to African continents, none of such principle had ever been seen nor even help to generally accept Africans whom the tour challenges of this

[18]   See, Marth. L. Cottam. Dieth-Uhler. Elena, M . Thomas. P, (2010) An

Introduction to political psychology, 2rd edition, pp324-327,

continent could be improved if we could fashion out possible and constructive attitude towards the people of the continents beyond our quest for exploitations beyond African thoughtful imaginations. The African people are often forgotten in the shadow of ingratitude, failures, poverty, underdevelopment, conflicts and constant's instability as their birth rights. This is even where most worlds are crying over the natures of African state's chaos. The essential support positively to secure Africans the needed stability had sometimes been distinguished as African problems. Sometimes, I think Africans leaders and its elites as those with the inability to understand the vision and the troubles of the nation they are preserved today, and as such they have failed themselves and those collectively under their control. I imagine intellectually that , The idea of democracy is philosophical terms that must not be baked from a foreign country. Preferably it should be seen as a mechanism under which the inhabitants of the states, continent, and regions could collectively negotiate their existence, agreed upon their minds, share their combined thoughts, vision with their own people irrespective of their linguistic differences, cultural differences and social mobility. However, hence, they found themselves in a defined territory. The leaders must act to define the liberty and freedom to its citizens under a defined negotiation made of what the groups of people collectively agreed as their fundamental laws by which their country's democratic ideals could be stretched to defend their own sovereignty against an outside

Aggression. This is what I think democratic thoughts should be conceived. It should be unfair, unjust for an external body to make its domestic laws to other continents through deceptive and false-fullness needs to other continents as the most accepted principle of different continent's existence. Even though, not even the United nation general assembly's resolution of the 1514 and 1960s, which called for granting of independence to the formal colonial African continent's independence couple with the resolutions of 1541, which applied the rights of self-determination to ethnically, culturally from the existing states in the African continent is enough to secure Africans the right to alter their fortune from the Western acrobatic politics and ideological democratic crafting. As Hitler will argue in his radical efforts to accept the Austrian Empire and parts of Czechoslovakian regions, noted that the existing frontiers were artificially created and did not reflect the identities of the people on either side of them. This position may have indicated why African regions are quite terrifying to administer as legal institutions, despite its long sustained as preserved colonial tools. Therefore, it must be correct to put forward the argument that for African democratic sustainability be achieved, the fundamental acceptance by both African and international communities must agree that the whole Africa today's is illegal institutions and as such, democratic sustainability should neither be expected nor be located in the African continents but what African and the external communities should be asking should currently are; how could we help Africans to construct their countries along their historic state establishment before the European eventual creation of the contemporary frontier's states? It is, therefore, thought that the world accepts these fundamental realities so that sustainable democratic constructed should be erected in African continents on the face of unworkable strategic policies formulated towards African countries since independence in the 60s without visible solutions to the human suffering under poverty, violence, wars and terrorism in the African continents. Besides, The West had established that African as far as history had recorded was classified as children and as such, doomed to no good if left responsible about themselves[19]. Thus, we could see this method of thinking as what eventually leads to the colonial interceptions by the name of exploitations instead of collective false argument the Africans were taught how to work through the European civilizations. It was even believed by the conquest of European naïve that given that Africans are unable to help themselves, should be taken by their well again, and shown the way they should go[20]. One influential argument which led King Leopold to single handily secure the entire Congo as his personal property despite that Congo twice more bigger than Brussel. Perhaps, The many false adventures of European in Africa ~~continent with their inability~~ to tell the truth about what good

[19]   Basil Davidson, (1964) the African past, the chronical from Antiquity to the

modern times.pp.265-274

[20]   Ibid,273

84

things there saw had rather brought African people and continents good faith but succeeded to bring for African people condemnation, seeing as deadly continents, poor and poverty riding continent. However, most of the same Europeans live honestly in many countries of Africans with their families, and most resources needed in Western Europe's are from African continents. Why cannot a sense of a good reasoning shape the West foreign policy to that the world could save place for all if they are deciding to facilitate the equal treatment of African continents and its resources in particular and industrious ways for a collective peace, unity, development, protection and sustainable democratic transitions and coordinated efforts to strengthening the continents without thinking about the dark age centuries ago? We may recall, Clapham, C. (1996) debates on the 'monopoly state' which has weak administrative structures, violent domestic opposition and a failing economy. The leaders of the state do not acknowledge the weakness of their positions, but rather use the machinery of the state to suppress or co-opt any opposition[21]. As well as the case of instability in Congo reflects historically, Mobutu was assisted by Western powers in his takeover of the state in 1965, and was helped by European nations and particularly the US throughout his rule. Predominantly, on the failures of Africans, It has often been argued E.g.; Jeffrey Herbst (1997) that

[21]   Clapham, C. 1996. Africa and the International System: the politics of state survival. Cambridge: Cambridge University Press.

in state collapse lie the seeds of a new kind of international society. Thus he argues: "A far more revolutionary approach would be for at least parts of Africa to be re-ordered around some organization other than the sovereign state. While such reforms would be a dramatic change in international society, their adoption would be an important acknowledgement of what is actually happening in parts of Africa where many states do not exercise sovereign authority over their territories[22]" Nevertheless, its most important that showing all reasons why democratic fruits could not be located in the continents in Africa, Davidson designates the nation state in Africa as a blasphemy or a handcuffs and asserts that the nation state in Africa does not liberate and protect its citizens, but that it is constrictive and exploitative. He predicts the future erosion of national boundaries both in Africa and in the world[23]. This assertion has paved the ways we see African continents today where corporate existence will never exist collectively among Africans people until such 'frontiers and fabricated' boundaries are dismantled, which could further pave ways for the universal waves of ushering stability in Africa. This demanding view I think could

---

[22] Herbs, J. 1997. Responding to State Failure in Africa, in Michael Brown, Owen Cote, Sean Lynn-Jones and Steven Miller (eds.) Nationalism and Ethnic Conflict. Cambridge, Massachusetts: The MIT Press.

[23] Davidson, B. 1992. The Black Man's Burden: Africa and the curse of the nation-state. London: James Currey.

be helped in resolving the buggies of difficult and frontier states created by African to find their respective destiny. Still, how could all the situation in African continents comes to end is simply a matter of the West accepting to remove their individual contribution in fostering disunity by continuing to foster damaging Western ideas in Africa, which had in large extends contributed significantly to the active various conflicts, consuming the continents through a dishonest policy towards the continent which already had enough share of political, societal and violence as its share of colonial fabrication? An illustration under which classical African stage of recovery could be discovered for the benefits of locating democratic necessities in Africa through African's ways of state's formation from their traditional historical makeup.

Stage Fourteen

Is African continent stagnant as predicted?

The Shifting Dimension in Africa States

How to face the African challenges!!!

Frankly, I will suggest that, there is no any specific species of novel attacks that could be installed for the contemporary challenges confronting the continent of African's states rather than to uproot the facet of the root causes of the continent's Un-settlement. Which mean, Africans must initiate a sort of a radical attempt at shutting down the gap separating the entire African race, people from their historical captive by the Western imperial design artificial donating Western values to Africans as democratic nations? I will indicate that Africans youth must pass up entirely to the preservation of the existing artificially stretched states in the contemporary phases of globalization. This symbolic step and efforts will help Africa to facilitate a form of discontinuation from the already cracked and fragile donated sovereign states to Africans. Without such a move to facilitate African's own state diagram, which could project African continent into a constructive development and stability, it will be very Harding for Africans to escaping constant conflict from generation to posterity. No doubt, this recommendation as a starting point to African re-discovery bringing them back into stability and progression. Unsteadily, given the unstructured states offer by the West to Africa people historically without an attempt by the international laws to losing its stamps on African separate groups to go on their separate path as it was during pre-colonial states, how could democratic development in the African continent be envisioned in the faces disorganized states fixed together for Africans? How then could Africans uproot these deadlock problems is very much unresolved impediments in Africa? The fact that scholars and analysts have drawn attention to various African dichotomies by labeling them as 'weak' or 'failed' state is, in that respect, only secondary (Hamre & Sullivan, 2002, p. 96, Shaibu, 2013). There have been fewer symbolic attempts to postulate a collective claim that the gravest dangers to the world safekeeping are no longer stretched specifically on the weapon of mass destruction nor the increment of military threats arising from the challenging, of a great power, but rather transcontinental threats stemming from ill and under satisfied ruled in most countries of the African continent. Especially, when look from a assorted articles arising from the Western sphere's decades after the 90s. E.g. Kaplan's influential 1994 Atlantic Monthly article, "The Coming Anarchy," which described state failure in West Africa and darkly predicted that it would spread throughout the world (Kaplan, 1994) Therefore, observing from these various dark indications arising from the continents of Africa as the threats to the global communities, what had the international community's nor institutions, specifically down to facilitate these burning issues be identified and resolved over the past centuries of several African nation states. This chapter traces the new shifting dimension shocking the African stability and further fostering a comprehensive instability in the continents instead chosen to stick to carrying on exploitative trades as a matter of 'usual strategies' towards the African continents. As we are mostly aware and had to acknowledge from but past and presents, various academic and scholarly contributions towards African state failures and changes had spread wide and distance as stretched above. Nevertheless, Baranyi and Powell (2005) argue that "conceptions of state fragility, weakness and failure coverage around two ideas." First, fragility refers to certain states' inability and/or unwillingness to provide essential public goods like security from external threats, rule of law and basic social services to most of their citizens. Second, fragility is a matter of degree - ranging from states that have ceased to exist in all, but names and cannot provide protection or welfare to anyone, to certain states that can deliver most public goods to most of their citizens24. Kofi Annan remarked before the Council on Foreign Relations in New York in 2004 that, "whether the threat is terror or aids, a threat to one is a threat to all. Our defenses are only as strong as their weakest link" (Annan, 2004). Thus, establishing this background, simply answered to all of us that the threat in Africa states as neither of wars, poverty, terrorism, state failures is problems for all international communities. The massive movements of most African citizens in the Western countries are carefully facilitated by the inconveniences in the different countries. This indicates that if most of the healthier young generations of Africans are well happy, and their lives secure by every facility needed to make them worthy of their continents, no one of African citizens will ever choose to come into with heavy discriminatory policies and traditions against them in most Europeans countries. This straightforward perspective should be acknowledged that the most switched ideology of the global community sucking African

---

[24] Baranyi S., and Powell, K., Fragile States, Gender Equality and Aid Effectiveness: A Review of Donor Perspectives, The North-South Institute,

continent. Thus, to these ends, the respective on African communities shifting across to Europe, which is very much hardly to secure only for the Africans and not the Western citizens going to Africa had rather creates more difficult situations for both the Africans and their Western counterpart. Still, for West to secure themselves with the mass intrusion of the Africans citizens who feel life's were too much disorganized back in their home countries is one fundamental difficulty for the human and national stability in the West without foreigners. Which I desirably hope that the ill state created in Africa and its constant protected often by the Western world and their African counterpart collaborators for their interest and for the benefits of those in power and their agents had two established African states on a unpararel democratic sustainability. Even so, as the numerous indications showed, for example. The resulting index of (Failed States Index) provides a profile of the new world disorder of the 21st century and demonstrates that the problem of weak and failing states is far more dangerous than generally believed. Approximately 2 billion people live in insecure states, with varying degrees of vulnerability to widespread civil conflict. Despite this inappropriate human suffering in some African continents, its seem irrelevant for the powerful Western countries to reduce their quest in African continent by seeing reasons to empower Africans with the sources of technological needed materials nor in spite of bringing closer technologies to African countries where raw materials are extracted so that this opportunity could help boost

African development as well as reducing high rates of African dependency on the Western good nor even help to stop African citizens to seek for greener pastures abroad. Consequently, despite most African challenges, the Western policy towards African continent has been rather harsh while often claiming the needs for the protection of human rights. For illustration design. In 1951, the EU started as a project intended to breathe life into the injured body of a continent mauled by the savagery of nationalistic hubris. The horrid trauma of a landscape filled with doom, and the very credible threat of its recurrence brought statesmen around to the then incredible proposal of surrendering part with their sovereignty to a supranational institution (Vernon, 1953:183) indeed, looking at the EU, for example, and most of their attempt to speak about human right protection and aspiration, what could there say about the death of most thousand people wasted European border managements over the years? For examples, on the 7th of October 2013 the EU added around 350 corpses to the mass grave that it has been piling up in the Mediterranean. These needlessly wasted lives speak not only about the EU's appalling border management. They should be taken as a warning of a far wider tragedy unfolding all across the EU. The dead African ~~migrants could be thought as~~ potentially dead EU citizens. This

---

25   **Rodrigo Bueno Lacy and Henk van Houtum** (December 5, 2013) **Europe's Border Disorder**

http://www.e-ir.info/2013/12/05/europes-border-disorder/

92

disregard for the African humanity may be seen as a dramatic result of the expanding disrespect for minorities all across the EU25. As the contemporary challenges of the African continents continues, its wide spread of the Africans lacking human rights. What then is the proper definition of human, accurately?

Stages Fifteen

Africa Reflection:

Theoretical Border of This Arguments

Rengger describes human right as "a mask for Western interests" (2011, 1173) which meaning another serious obstacle for universal human rights is the claim that it is a new form of imperialism. Additionally, Samir Amin recognizes the human rights agenda as shallow rhetoric disguising the promotion of US interests (2004, 78). The human rights discussion surrounding the 2003 invasion of Iraq has justified the fear that human rights are a tool of neo-imperialism, particularly as the US has not promoted human rights in Kuwait despite years of presence there (Amin, 2004, 77). Also In: Ramcharan, 2008, 16). The basis of rights needs not to have cultural or philosophical origins, but instead be a response to common injustice's humanity has seen (Ramcharan, 2008, 17). Ramcharan believes the Horowitz's argument shows "humanity's collective experience with injustice constitutes a fruitful foundation on which to construct a theory of rights" perhaps, until 'Cultural differences and the right to self-determination must be taken into account for human rights to be applied (Mutua, 2008, 34), otherwise they will be irrelevant or rejected as imperialism. They have been a dramatic shift towards how we saw the phrases the ' passing out of colonialism' beyond man nods, some fundamental issues were at most still in active in preventing African's full realization of their continental wealth's. For examples, Martin J. Wiener (2013) advance an extension of argument on colonialism by a fourfold inheritance from colonialism: first, of authoritarian state structures and habits, with "emergency" laws readily employable in suspend liberties; second, by economic structures created to facilitate foreign exploitation of the nation's resources; third, by colonial authorities' promotion of religious and ethnic distrust; and finally, by ongoing international political and economic relationships and structures emerging out of colonialism designed to preserve and maintain this pernicious colonial inheritance—that is, by "neocolonialism[26]." In the same vein, Samir Amin, declared in 2010, "Colonization was very catastrophic and hence the world economic order should be held responsible for any post-independence failures[27]." Thus, at the post-colonialism, the music

---

[26]   *Martin J. Wiener (2013)* the Idea of "Colonial Legacy" and the Historiography of Empire, **Journal of the Historical Society.** Volume 13, Issue 1, pages 1–32, March 2013

[27]   *Ibid 1*

of Africa wrangling for joy could rather be astonished by Basil Davidson, on his remarked in his admiring 1973 biography of Kwame Nkrumah, the "dish" the new leaders were handed on the day of independence "was old and cracked and little fit for any further use. Worse than that, it was not an empty dish. For it carry the junks and jumbles of the century of colonial muddle and 'make it to do,' and this is new. . . Ministers had to accept along with the dish itself. What shone upon its supposedly golden surface was not the reflection of new ideas and ways of liberation, but the shadows of old ideas and ways of servitude[28]. On this still on these feet, Africans are wounded beyond apology. The control of human continues to enslave with arrogant and tricks are gradually fading off the surface of the sky. Even so, the truth must be told by Africans who really suffered the pains of injustices but in a fair play dimension.

Stages Sixteen

The African Journey so Far;

Between Growths & Sovereignty;

In the face of several Africans assorted acrimonious in both past and present being calculated and position for the Africans in form 'inferior greeds over the past decade. In the present day 21st

---

[28]   *See Basil Davidson,* Black Star: A View of the Life and Times of Kwame Nkrumah *(*London: James Currey, 1973), 94.

century, one wonders if such unmerited injustices around the globe done to the African continent and people truly worth it to be reserve consciously for African race? This thoughtful message which may have emanated from political deceptions, acrobatic trade manipulations, and foreign policy tightly related to formal colonizers, foreign media's open eyes ball on African with negative impressions, which were often expressed with connections to how Africans can never help but to continue the dependency on the foreign aids. However, matters arising from the Western countries at the closer look after post-colonialism was done with a higher percentage of vibration of new methods to hold African accountable through an invisible ideology or rather call it a completely democratic dishonest of the human race that most Africans leaders are corrupted and therefore, are incapable of delivering themselves from their deposited dependency level by the Western countries. Difficultly, how true could an African accept this Western view? May we even ask that which Western countries could claim ever to do business with African people without his being the first to offer ideas of 'gift' in pursuance to their interest? Indeed, No African leaders with a clear conscience could decline these claims despite their efforts to neither denial nor notwithstanding accepts, in principle, as standard gifts. Still, those gifts are recorded by the West as corrupts and bribed without African leaders noticed, until African realized it is enough, achieved these phenomena as impediments to their growths, peace and stability while, in public office, African states will continue to be serving their formal colonial interest instead of their citizens indoctrinated poverty and converted violence in African continents in Western pursuance to their various interests. This picture of African continent's design by the Western media and its collaborators. In my own opinion, justices demand collective moral thoughts that there are times for everything under the face of the death which the Western technocrats, media and policies most realized. That Africans had suffered so much the causes of violence, racism, despotism in their country, which was never their designs nor establish such a harsh policy, but 99% of what is pounding most Africans into their early burial graves are Western collective design to tag's Africans as their personal property despite the so called 'artificial' independence that most Africans were granted. In fact, Africans are human beings, and it is getting to painful moments that Africans will at someday faces the West to explain their sympathy to Africans after hundreds of years in their bags. In keeping with reality, I mention some place in this book how aids, to Africans, false democracy, international laws are all directed to African's countries as the most compliances as global laws. What made them international laws, which granted some groups of country's rights to some extend uprooted some generation of the human races from the world, none of them created, but being born as everyone else and meet them inside without the consents of those people? How many Africans were negotiators towards the acceptances of international laws, and such laws are being kept by all signatories? Africans are being directed to take aids after the same groups of countries had collaborated to disorganize any government of African's leaders who refuses to dance to their invisible master's tune of strategies. For example, Egypt directly became terrorist safe havens under the turn that it must be democratic today, Tunisia, Libya, Syrians, Mali, and the Central African Republic etc. as many incidents could indicate that an African idea towards liberating their people are often dangerous and, which will endanger millions of Africans into the death. For example, Africans attempt to see aids to most African campaign took other directions from the Western media as it was quote, E.g. In the May 22 edition of the *Financial times* aid activists were paraded out revealing panic "at the prospect that (Ms. Moya's) ideas are gaining traction, Jeffrey Sachs, the U.S. academic and aid advocate, accused her of endangering lives. Her ideas he said are 'absolutely pernicious and could lead to the deaths of millions of people.[29] "also, around this logical different frame periods, specifically in the May 8 edition of the Rwandan daily the New times she wrote: "At the height of the 15th Genocide Commemorations, the director of Human Rights Watch, Kenneth Roth, published a rather mocking if not provocative article given

---

[29] *JEHRON MUHAMMAD,* (**JUN 30, 2009**) is Africa throwing off the yoke of dependency.

http://www.finalcall.com/artman/publish/Perspectives_1/Is_Africa_throwing_o ff_the_yoke_of_dependency.shtml the timing of the publication and the title, 'The Power of Horror in Rwanda.' Therefore, in pursuance to realistic issues on the ground, "Roth in his article penned at a deeply emotional time for Rwandans deliberately seeks to change the subject from their history, their plight and suffering to laying the credence to revisionism. "And so while he acknowledges the great economic progress and development by the Rwandan government, he suffers selective amnesia as to how good governance is the main ingredient for economic growth," she argued[30]. It is my observation that, despite Africans deeply concentration to preserve nor totally uproots the impediments holding the Africans constantly on the ground, the Western government instead of looking the side pain of the most African poverty, instability to active and validate a program for accepting the African's shift to their human fact. They choose to neglect every effort put in places by Africans as those catastrophes and could endanger African developments. The westerns are not African God. So, it is getting closer to a period where each man, woman and children of the prophet should face their own idiosyncratic domestic problems instead of stretching their necks in causing revolutions around the world. Africans suffered beyond reasoning's and I will argue that the means for the African current situations is to turn to themselves and ask questions 'why are still here and where next to go alone in the cause of our human liberty without advisers from external bodies who also had their own share of worldly problems. The

---

[30]   Ibid 4

African dimension I could undoubtedly see is that African youths must reject the un-ending domination of their continents by foreign governments and policy makers, but this view should be carefully studied that it does not mean close business contact with the West, but to get involved in any kind of business on equal terms without one offer to bribe or give delightful gifts as friendships in terms of collective engagements. It is believed that no countries are an island. Thus, Africans should be unfastened to the world as each region opens its gateways to your entry. It should rather be an equal dimension of human understanding without one media nor government focus on one region as threats to the rest of the world. *It is at the heart of this book that international laws should be re-instituted in a democratic protocol where every single nation should collectively know their limits in terms of any aggressive movements to other man sovereign countries.* As it is currently on the region's of Central African Republic, where the French militaries are killing African citizens in the names of the rebel. I believe conflict resolutions do not involve a machine gun or weapons of mass destruction? African must see reasons to learn the hard lessons of their lives under one collective dream as black continents. The West, in fact, had done their best to African continents, but Africans believe it is CAPITALLY enough to change that un-ending diabolical and promising backing with weapons, aids and other inconveniencing policies for Africans to accept. This book demands that African must take their space in the global politics as the leader's not dependent societies from one generation to another. The Africans had been crushed into the bottom of oppression also being isolated economically through equal trading policies, politically through various manipulations, culturally by creating differences among the multi-ethnic groups in Africa, and by democratically forcing Africans to the ideas as a universal policy for the world reconciliation even when the West realized that the people of dissimilar cultures, traditions are not the same in both socially, politically and in all aspect of human life's, they still stick their conventional crafting to foists their own wills on the Africans people and their land through sanctions and embargoes. The questions now is rather weathered the world democracies are viewing the complicated human sufferings the regions of African continents as a result of multi-national companies, aid damages to African development and self-reliance, conflict engineered by creating divisions around the continent by various interest groups? Even as the atmosphere of injustice seems to not dwarfing completely, as Madiba Mandela will would observe, the African people do not need a degree before they recognize the collective injustice hammered on them by the few groups of the minority whites who intruded their beautiful land with both biblical and gunpowder for their own aggrandizement to obstruct their personal liberty and freedom. So also, one wonder if the modern Africans youth does not need a degree nor be told about the un-ending human poverty in African continents which was a design from an external force disproof them their rightful existence as humans, the legitimate realization of all unimaginative wealth of their nations but rather but to serve other nation's citizens. So, the Western ideological crafting at the aftermath of post-colonialism had continued to post-dating the African realistic liberty, freedom, justice to the free ownership of what their lands provided to them as free gifts of the natures of which Africans hands will never conquer such power in other continents. *What kind of unfairness is beyond this pragmatic dichotomy?* (Shaibu,2014) As Thomas Jefferson wrote in June of 1776, which then, unfortunately, John Adams, Benjamin Franklin and other delegates to the Continental Congress took out of the Declaration of Independence: "He note [The King of England] has waged cruel war against human nature itself, violating its most sacred rights of life and liberty in the persons of a distant people [Africans] who never offended him, captivating and carrying them into slavery in another hemisphere, to incur miserable death in their transportation thither [to America]." Look at how well Mr. Jefferson wrote what England did, because England was the culprit that introduced us into this hemisphere, and started the Trans-Atlantic Slave Trade[31]" furthermore, in attempt to clarify the fundamental issues of depriving African's American rights and liberty, *Abraham Lincoln continued:* "Such separation, if ever effected at all, must be

[31]   LOUIS FARRAKHANN, (*DEC* 10, 2013) 'SEPARATION! Independence!
http://www.finalcall.com/artman/publish/Minister_Louis_Farrakhan_9/article_101034.shtml

102

effected by colonization; and no political party, as such, is now doing anything directly for colonization. Party operations at present only favour or retard colonization incidentally. The enterprise is a difficult one; but 'when there is a will there is a way'; and what colonization needs most is a hearty will. 'Will' springs from the two elements of moral sense and self-interest. Let us be brought to believe it is morally right, and, at the same time, favourable to, or, at least, not against, our interest, to transfer the African to his native clime, and we shall find a way to do it, However, high the task may be. The children of Israel, to such as to include four hundred thousand fighting men, went out of Egyptian bondage in a body." Ideologically, *I will argue that the both men of wisdom acknowledge the needs for equal parade ground between the two races (black and whites) and also give them equal opportunity to each one to see if truly the blacks are in fact they are children who do not want to grow as suggested by early Western historians. It is all about an illusion which had to lead the Western world into anarchy suffered through the two world wars. Time to re-think on African continents because the pot is almost full of water and it might at some point flow backward (Shaibu, 2013 December)*

Thus, the subsequent inquiry will look critically at the key puzzles that apply to how do China appear to Africa in the contemporary world politics? The point examines below account for mixed reactions about how the Chinese tries to engage African continent and with a specific amount of considerable debates on the emerging global chase for economic recovery towards Africa.

Stages Seventeen

African & China's Mix-reaction:

'The Global Political Questions of our times'

Summary:

We may off our shoes and said Africans have been chained beyond recovery in the faces of global Western powers on how Africans nations could huddle their prosperity as far as the continent remain a multi-cultural societies. Yet, how long could such accession hold against African continent and peoples? Especially when the contemporary issues of Chinese signal in African continents come in the context of geopolitical landscape exploration. Even so, how could such an approximation about African people with Chinese in African is explained outside a mere dilution that the continent is in another controversial ends by the emergence of Chinese in Africa once more? This second coming of Chinese in African continent may have been recognized by many intellectuals and other international affairs commentators as complex as further framed as 'neo-imperialism' extra than for the prospect of securing Africans the considered necessary developments of their natural resources? But, does such view mark another African transition hooked on as extra endless subjugation? The above ground new era of Chinese in Africa is well challenged from *political standpoints, economic realities, domestic in-capacitation, ideological predictions, strategic partnership etc.* as each of these sections is well delivered comprehended from political, psychological expectations and theorizations.

Stages eighteen

Africans Partnership:

The 'Mix-Reaction' About the Chinese
'The chain of Ground UN-expectation in the world politics'

Is Africa experiencing a new shift of political partnership and graph in Africa? Perhaps, this view may have to establish steps towards closing the section and stages of Europeans Formula 'one' in African civilizations. Although, we may have observed a kind of signal in Africa recently, which has an open letter towards what might seem ends of artificial truth about the states of an African journey in the recent development programs undertaking by African development banks and support from the Chinese government. Even so, for the majority of the international community, everything seems like a dream that was never expected soonest. We may understand this position by how the Western media sees Chinese in Africa. Especially, those being manipulate by the foreign media as the only key to a fading face of Africa without knowing that Africans are experiencing a sort of a new beginning for the Africans continents to utter their historical captivity by the Europeans subjugation. Conceivably, this imaginary conclusion may have echo accurately from the broad-spectrum of public view as down-to-earth, but from the African tears of hope image, many of these accessions are entirely false wrapping up, but then, what about the mix-reaction of Chinese in African at the close of 20th century? Have African ground expectations been secured for their posterity surviving from dependency, and the continuing cycles of poverty and under-developmental experimentations. As observed recent Harries, (1975) he quotes . . . An understanding of contemporary Africa. . . Can only be advanced by making a radical departure from the assumptions and modes of study associated with [the] conventional wisdom . . . The political and economic life of the African states cannot be adequately understood if we restrict our analysis to internal or domestic factors within the individual states (Harris, 1975s: vii)[32]. Thus, in viewing African from a painful psychological perfectives (Shaw, 1974) reinforce that African Politics can be best explained, then, by concentrating on the linkages between 'external' and 'internal' actors: a truly 'radical' perspective are based on the premise that the political economy and international status of each state are mainly determined through relations at this interface[33]. Perhaps, the focus on the central linkages between the Chinese interest in Africa continent and its foreign associates for examples, Brazil, India, South Korea, Japan, etc., are crucial relationship which this section analyzes because it has historically been neglected and thus it does not yet to receive appropriate pragmatic and abstract consideration. Still, as the questions of Chinese in African has expanded beyond regional geopolitics and had a drawer a wider context today's as

---

[32]   **See Also**, Amin, S. (1972): 'Underdevelopment and Dependence in Black Africa - Origins
          .and 525.

[32] **See**, seminar on Non-capitalist Development in Africa in Helsinki in August 1976 and at the annual conference of the African Studies Association in Boston in November 1976. (Markovitz, 1977: 25-97; Shaw, 1977b).

[32] Carmody and Taylor, 2010, qote in Scoones, Lidia and H. Tugendhat 2013, IDS Bulletin vol.44, number 4, july 2013

          New   Delopment   Encounters;   China   and   Brazil   in   African Agriculture.Contemporary Forms,' Journal of Modern African Studies 10, 4

          (December): 503-525.

[33]   **See**, seminar on Non-capitalist Development in Africa in Helsinki in August 1976 and at the annual conference of the African Studies Association in Boston in November 1976. (Markowitz, 1977: 25-97; Shaw, 1977b)

critical problems to most Western global hegemony, even so, one of the blind difficulties belong to the African leader's inability to respond to the technical demand for their internal domestic fragilities over the past decade and this situation had to detail the constant foreign engagement on the African continent enduring Greenland and resources for foreign significance which in logical footsteps Chinese had followed since the fourteen century contacts with African people. A significant part of this has focused on 'resources' diplomacy'[34]. Which had to establish Chinese ideological diplomacy towards occupying African state natural resources to sustain their massive population and domestic economic sustainability? Undoubtedly, this issue has been argued recently that, in 2012, the Sino-African trade with the Chinese had escalated to reach its highest top gear in the continent development historically above that of the elsewhere Western counterpart who penetrate African continents with strategic democratic logic as 'Aid for African development and security' at reaching nearly US$200 billion according to official Chinese documentation (Yan, 2013). Still, the Chinese transition in African continent had a positive effect in the African continent, but with everlasting economic and institutional dependency on Chinese cheap resources which neither last nor had positive values for the African historical demands over the past decade. African continents have enormously

---

[34]   Carmody and Taylor, 2010, qote in Scoones, Lidia and H. Tugendhat 2013, IDS Bulletin vol.44, number 4, july 2013
        New Delopment Encounters; China and Brazil in African Agriculture.

twisted a huge influential diplomacy for the Chinese growth internationally as well as providing abundant food and energy security for the Chinese government. No doubt, Chinese foreign relation had skyrocketed into every Conner of African countries in search of every available, reserve resources to explore to their country nation states economic growth. As we could see, for example, the Chinese import bank alone had lent roughly US$67.2 billion to sub-Saharan Africa between (2001 and 2010) a sum quoted by M. Cohen, 2011 to be higher than that of the Western. While the Chinese engagement in Africa may have signaled a mixed reaction from both domestic entrepreneurs and the external Western complex diplomacy to the African continent, the truth remains that between 1949 to around 2006-7; Chinese disbursement has been estimated to have reached the values of US$ 5.6 billion[35]. The values of which had provided African space to trade their domestic resources as well as an exchange of technological advancement to African people and society as compare better to that of Western string attachment to aids and democracy in Africa in exchange for exploitation without development.

Stages Nineteen

The Chinese Commercial Undertaking in Africa;
Reemerging cold war's in Africa?

---

[35]   See, Davies, 2006.

Although, it has been argued practically that the relations between the China and the African's continent has been highlighted from the historic engagement. This is a fact because there is some specific evidence of the early trade connections which eventually highlights traces of medieval contacts around the 14th century, which had Somehow related to the tribes of Cape Town's of South Africa north claimed there is a descendant of Chinese sailors during the 13th century. However, their physical outer shell is parallel to the contemporary Chinese with paler skin and a Mandarin sounds tonal language. All the same, these groups in the southern African name themselves as "abandoned people", Awatwa in their language[36]. However, in the recent times, increase domestic demands in China with a massive population had to re-validate their historic commitments to exploit African resources have been injured and further being neglected to develop by the Western countries. This shift ground has to usher in Chinese technical diplomacy, especially if we look at the rate under which the Chinese commercial bank loans to African complemented to about 20-30-years concessional loans from the Export-Import Bank of Chinese's Government. All such loans to 'un-attached strings were to be utilized on the key technical cooperation

---

[36]   See, http://www.china.org.cn/world/2009-11/09/content_18849890.htm

mandate of resources development with strategic turn over the Chinese domestic interest. We could also see that Chinese in Africa ideological needs back home were traded with Africa logically in the name of development, but not as Western counterpart may have a design as aids to the Africans as poor to the extent under which the Chinese has almost securely every African country signature on a different contract with heavy returns for their domestic common interest. *For example,* the Chinese premier note in 2009; "China has never attached any political strings to its support and assistance to Africa, and nor will it do so in the future[37]". *His political speech may interpret as the Chinese continue involvement in Africa may have come to stay from the present to the historic posterity without giving out a chance for any country's competition in Africa resources.* Still, how should Africans understand such an acrobatic smart shot on African resource exploitation? I often recommend, the Chinese may have established ideological trade mark under which she has label African continent as their personal property as the Western experiences over a decade has shown the entire African continent that Africans are not matching colleagues of Europeans. But still African needs to understand that Chinese with relatives cheap

---

[37]   Full text of Wen's speech at 4th Ministerial Conference of FOCAC; Xinhua, November 9, 2009,

   http://www.china.org.cn/world/2009-11/09/content_18849890.htm

loans may have attracted their most selfish ends politically but how long will such loans, exploration of Chinese in African will sustain African beyond the burden of debt and luxury of cheap resources is one thing African must take note. Even though as expected by most Western countries for the Chinese government to publish its stewardship publicly from Africa without any visible responses from the Chinese people Republic, the Chinese strategic dilemma is that there are not readily interested to envision such need but rather choose to publish only their growing financial luxury to the African continents with a different figure as there often may choose or decided to make public. For example, at most, all modern argument by Chinese in African continent are placed on the importance of agricultural landmarks in line with the Chinese economic transformation agenda domestically. *At most, central to this ideology lies the strategic philosophy encoded by the Chinese domestically on how to explore African resources, but with the technique of trading cheap transformation with less operational technology in Africa in exchange for un-quantifiable crude oil, gold mining, Agricultural soil fertility, techniques and textures back for their domestic survival (Saibu 2013).* This argument may have contradicted the ideological position of most Chinese intellectual who had subscribed to nailing African continent in hot demand of China's selfless support to African development, peace and sustainability (Shaibu, 2014). I often suggest that even if the African's people may have produced a weak institution capable of

112

dividing us complete the black countries, but what I see could secure African integration beyond being used by several world emerging and the past Western hegemony is to first secure for African people need for moral re-union in line with African traditions as the key point to transform the whole African society. This is key because the root of inequality syndrome, Godfatherism, political deception, division between father and sons-in-law may have been already established in Africa and regularly been polish by technical ideologies in Africa over the years. But the truth of the matter is that unless, African countries, political elites reduce their quest for wealth, inequality syndrome, political deception, identity politics, hatred among themselves as black people, African continents will continue to suffer detrimental exploitations from various external forces. Maybe one day, African will be transferred to Vietnamese to be colonized. (Shaibu, 2014). Therefore, most trade deals in Africa call it, development dichotomy, common selfless service, empowerment, technology transfer, a struggle to liberate African continent from dependency nor diplomatic partnership to secure Africans as a global geo-strategic continent, the African continent has been known ever before colonialism as 'pivotal to the world economy liberation'. So, the model of re-shaping ideology towards African people by cruelty languages fabricated to the individual countries aggrandizement in Africa is not new and therefore perfectly go well with into what I will call *'Chinese blind strategy in African civilization'*. Many of the Chinese ideas to Africa continents are those framed in line with intervention policy, a technique used by George Bush Jr to make safe Iraq's oil wealth for the US domestic significance. Considerably, the Chinese economic realities are also framed in a shadow of my proposed term *'Imperial outfit'* a symbol necessary for the Chinese economic survival, which had in the past formed as the sufficient struggle envision by the West, Indians, Brazils to relate with the African continent. If technically I am true to the African vs Chinese realities in Africa, the burden of African had not been neither structured according to the history of African people beyond exploitation which may had lead Africans to demands for their independence in the 60s and as such, sub-Saharan Africa is divided by interest on who need what, how do you wish to attract such needs, method of extraction are the whole strategic policies dominating relationship with the African people. 'Their resources are very essential for our domestic values, internal-wellbeing, trade, economic growth, but the development of their continents depends on African people. *How else do African people want to secure the means to understand that No nations of the world is interested in developing their domestic fragile institutions?* It is my intellectual view that, until the African stage, an adage fashion by Madiba Mandela in the 60s as "Enough is Enough" of inequalities to our nations and people, any democratic transformation by African elites seek to participate as key to their foreign policy, strategic advancement without the knowledge of how to secure their continent's equality of strategic development, trade exchange; it will be accepted as just an approval of poverty in magnificence landscape. I will argue that economic transformation, democratic relevance's, participatory development demands 'there is no universal law. But, where they are lovingly for equality of unity, integration and development among dissimilar nations, one could at extreme found human justices to be those of equality of purpose, objectives, advancement etc. Without which there is not something like human right safeguard as universal laws set off for the spirit of unique peace and tranquillity for the world stability (Shaibu, 2014)

Stages Twenty

The African Domestic Break-down;
An extra trial of 'Transformation from dependency?'

Elsewhere in the African history, it was verified that …the British owns the entire vast key wealthy and strategic world landscape as its personal property for over 200 years. Still, in the 21st century, such powers and enslavement of the human soul of humanity had been reduced to a common comradeship in both by designs or wars respectively. However, a positive search for the reasons behind such demands of hegemony rest with the British domestic and empire hegemony from the context of international affairs perfectives.. No doubt, the encroachment of the universe race as 'inferior' were not seen as African trademark alone, but even the history of the United States of America holds the same captivity. As the background above indicates, Chinese in Africa holds also the reverse certificate of an empire building back home as a key to their foreign policy and as many, African continents, weak states match its strategic echo especially at the backdrop of the Western moderns democratic liberalization of the African continent is deteriorating them due to their string policy of unfair attached to their African counterpart. This may have suggested Chinese quick stretch to Africa in the form of compensating Africans and as well healing the continents from the pressure of the Western dependency policies. In this way, adoption of the policy of non-attachment trade relations with African states, soft loan, technological exchange, educational training, road development, social facilities construction, etc are positioned to only attract the African released from holding stiff to their arrows, but then repairing Africans burden does not matter to the Chinese win-win policy to the African states. It is a thoughtful argument of this book that if African should ever be efficient in pursuing a significant burden of their past, positive challenges most be decorated to validate their pursuance to any strategic policy envision by the both neither Chinese nor its Western alliance. This because none of those nations are interested in developing African beyond what their domestic demands required in partnership with the African people. The African has been historically manipulated, organized with a negative expression, harmful interest and as well as establishes an extraordinary language to keep fine-turning African stages of development as unworthy and insignificant. It is my conviction that African most fasten their energy to facilitating a strong courage to build African states with what they have instantly instead of seeking abundant debt for their selfish aggrandizement in the name of transforming the continents from the Chinese game plan development in the African continent. Empirical evidence suggests that nations that flourish supported themselves locally without any form of branding their countries with debt and loans for private uses. Thus, the negative prospect for most current Chinese in African is hardly to be seen nor but history will surely judge those African leaders who decided to steal their country's wealth for their individual usages at the detriments of their country states poverty, underdevelopment, insecurity, un-unemployment and backwardness. I should also suggest that dialogue with the domestic difficult situation in African states should form only the basis under which vision of development could be initiated in the Africa trade with the Chinese questions in Africa. Indeed, it has been a ground expectation by the Chinese that African has finally being secured for their common one domestic interest, deep thought that the continent of African hard emerge after the historic turnaround of the West as states without historic structures nor memory and as such, they have technically rolled out any challenges from the African people. But, this view has a low and relatively poor significance to the majority of African intellectuals. For instance, As captured by Timothy Shaw and Malcolm Grieve, (1977)[38] and the other scholars of Africa's political economy who are troubled by the African past, present and future impact of dependence and inequalities. Given the false starts (Dumont, 1968), the lack of growth or redistribution (Davidson, 1974), and the underdeveloped class structures of African states, the trend is now towards 'de participation' (Kasfir, 1976: 14-27; Huntington and Nelson, 1976) or centralization along with coercion rather than to 'modernization' or 'development'; the 'traditional' paradigms 'resurrected' by Klinghoffer (1973) and Rubin and Weinstein (1974). Nevertheless, in any fashion possible the Chinese in Africa may have perceived the continents officially decorated by the West historically as weak institution and had no clue on how to blend change of tactics from their current existing system to magnetize their confusions ideologies to secure African wealth. Yet, I saw all the intrigues in African the African's elite's inability to change towards a sense of moral values to their domestic decays, power structures, values and visions for the direction proceed decade after post-colonialism. Consequently, in the absence of real domestic progress as strategies for development, then, the issues of integration into a sort of a global economy are perceived to be leading to the international policies of

[38] Dependence or Development: International and Internal Inequalities in Africa, *Development and Change, 8* (1977), 377408

compromise and to national regimes of cruelty (see Frank, 1972a, b and c; Galtung, 1971; O'Brien, 1975; Foster-Carter, 1974; Cardoso, 1972; Alschuler, 1976) Shaibu, 2014). These substances may even one day force many Africans states against the Chinese policy in Africa to be uprooted. What therefore should be recognized as the political groundwork of the Chinese neo-imperial strategy in African political institutions? In the case of nearly everyone African countries, it is the acknowledgement of African societal system as a continent succeeded by elites whose key interest is *'Quest for wealth creation'* which could be found around the political power corridor by the a small amount of elites whose obvious task were psychologically developed on the back shelf of a foreign interest, an extension of what crown the Chinese strategic neo-imperial-capitalist mega into Africa acceptable. Indeed, because the political elites in Africa are for all intents and purposes reliant on dependency and not within their internal resources, but they accept an external 'prop up' politics rather than on their visions domestically. Consistently, despite the long history of the dilemmas inherent in Chinese –African collaboration, The Africa's leaders are seeing is positioned at a standstill armchairs seeking for only short-term gains individually through contracts signatory with the Chinese external relations. Given these tactic backgrounds, a recognition of faith as a visible explanation for the Chinese interest in African recourse could not be attained by both the pathology of developing the African resources, nor its elusiveness natural history of exploitations in the fashion name of

African growth, this situation has being why such instantaneous universal medication establishes as relevant by the Chinese in Africa remain switched

Stages twenty-one

Ideological Predictions Outside African States;
Chinese in the Lens of Western Intricacy

As the questions of Chinese in Africa continents had dramatically turned into another cold war in Africa Geopolitics between the West-who as the elsewhere formal colonizers and the benefit of the essential Africans commodity for a century without a single gratification over the past decade of the Western civilizing Africans. Although, one thing remain significant in the 'Western' democratic ideology that has being coin among several Western countries for examples, the "West conditionality on everything to Africa, selectivity on how aid or utilizes their projects in Africa towards achieving double returns on each Euro spent in African's state and to uphold their historic colonial tricks in Africa. But, as we could observe in the modern Africa, the Western holding tight of Africans continent as still their property through a variety of conditionality, trade acrobatic policies, selectivity project and tighten boundary of solidarity to African continent had to usher in Chinese government who in a fair and realistic sense are not interested to championing Africans economic and political salvation but the Chinese policy towards Africans states are those mechanized, calculated ideologically through a thoughtful beliefs over years that capturing African wealth's could only be possible through throwing in heavy investment to Africans but with a cheap products, less expensive, less durability, less longevity, lack quality wise, call it sub-standard etc. having observe that Africans needs to explore an alternative region to sales their domestic trades and resources outside of the Western captivity. This has been the focal justification of the huge Chinese investment to the African continent. Again, this ideology is groundwork of policy design and laid out in the garden of the Chinese's empire as strategic significance to provide cheap resources for African states to help boost their economy, help strengthen their massive vast population back home. As Maureen F. M-chugh would observe, "In my experience, ideology is a lot like religion, it is a belief system and most people cling to it long after it becomes clear that their ideology does not describe the real world"[39]. In most realistic confession, African has been as matters of "and was designed consistently into a death court-martialed dependency on an illusion. Of course, in the context of the above explanation, It is my conviction that to 'un-packaged' the Chinese range of the political, economic, ideological game diagram in Africa. We need to understand how the Chinese indeed, domestically perceived the

---

[39]   *Half the Day Is Night* (1994)-
http://www.locusmag.com/1999/Issues/10/McHugh.html

peoples of Africa during the colonial and post-colonialism. The wider proximity with Africans dates back to the 50s and the long these perceptions about African have considerable to say about the Chinese traded Confucianism ideology in African who has much to do with patience and endurance, which may have in a larger scope have been framed by the contemporary Chinese dynamic-ism in African countries in what numerous Western countries consider as the Chinese imperial power or the emerging power in Africa. In an attempt to discuss much questions about why imperial questions becomes a constant identity with African most papulous economy of the world as African? Most of this reason could be linked to one of the classic question asked by the Congolese philosopher V. Y. Mudimbe when he said, " How was African Invented in the first place? His simple answer was " according to Mudimbe, is that the idea of Africa was initially fashioned not by Africans, but by non-Africans, as a 'paradigm of difference'. Africa, in other words, has served as an exotic prism through which outsiders, mainly Europeans, refracted images of 'the other' and of themselves. Therefore, if understand this point, it is possible that the modern idea of Africa emerged, in so many ways, mostly from the past, but those with a figure link with the dehumanizing crucible of Atlantic slavery. Hardly remain difficult to be uprooted from African despite the conventional logics of independence in the 60s. However, if we start to acknowledge from a moral sense of justices, one will finally arrive a logical conclusion that the problems of Neither China in Africa, neocolonialism, frontier states in Africa were all connected to the content under an act that the whole Africa itself was a subject design by out of un-clear visions by the Europeans about Africa. Which I may choose to assemble as imagination of black people as that of inferior Africa so cheap to be subjected to any kind of cruelty and injustices and further forged by an idea of collective domestic interest rather than those fashions in African realities.

Stages twenty-two

The Chinese Ideological Predictions in Africa;

'Power Behind the Fence in Africa Geopolitics'

"One truth about African continent perhaps, as a well disturbing of all realities is 'Every man and woman outside African state is known to be 'African messiah'. There all know African solutions and problem. Yet, none could nor rather fashion out a recognized solutions to this deficiency. Nevertheless, every interest and abuses portray to the African people and states are in essence of finding measures to secure African wealth. (Shaibu, 6th, 2014)

One extraordinary challenges in the 21st century may not be the symbol concerning the global energy scarcity, global warming, mass of weapon destruction nor even the questions of terrorism as a global enemy, but the emerging signal that the Chinese has chosen to re-occupied African continents has produced another global prediction over what is the strategic transitions of the Chinese in African resources to the global food security, energy security, cheap labour, free trade zones etc. still, how are this ideas being spread out globally? For instance, The Chinese in Africa lacks human right attendance, poor rehabilitations to African economy, facilitating corruptions in Africa, mechanizing security threat to African states, reducing African job opportunities, taking over African market etc. But when we look closely beyond artificial predictions as we have done during that dark ages and towards the ends of post-colonialism where Africans had not being given equal opportunity in almost all the needs of African people, one comes to wonder how did the global community whose major resources comes from African poor countries should be installed and logically should look at Africans? We can solve problems of inhumanity to humanity with the same hands that create them. Then, if we must react, we must be ready to clean our hands beyond recognition of our past. The most acceptable of all is that, we must accept a new shift of awareness within us as equal human creatures. I picture suggested being a true democratic transitions in facing human realities (Shaibu, 2014). thereafter, the Chinese relevance's in African may have surprises the global leaders whose interest are being tempered nor terminated to use the contemporary statistics means that we must re-examine why has the Chinese are succeeding in Africa despite their so call sub-standard quality product to African states. Yet, no country could deny the Chinese goods in the respective countries market. Nevertheless, one things we must understand from the Chinese ideological trade in Africa is that they have work very hard to smuggle African from dependency politically conditionality which had seen African states turn into another re-occupation by the formal colonizers but there is one difference here we must acknowledge about the Chinese in Africa, there are blending their own exploitative grappling in African states by showing some practical difference to African most enduring continents to see in practical forms. They encourage transfer of technology to most African states while still seating on the fence extracting oil and other natural resources to boosting their domestic desperate needs. The Chinese as we may not be aware are doing everything humanly possible to dominate African continent for the next two centuries to come. For example, However, their long term contracts often-15 years in some cases could signify that their policy towards African state is yielding gains and interest for their domestic utilization. Also, there is other terms of which the Chinese are building African through integration policy to influence their global strategic interest by the enduring ideological interpretations. Although, the Chinese understood too very carefully the global interest in Africa and there in some context racket around the foot-print of the Western pushing in African resources demands but with a different suitcase maybe advance beyond the Western perceptions and predictions.

The above discussion may have captured another sense of the cold war between the global powers in Africa .But as African proverbs will quote "Where two lion fights, its only the grasses that suffered the pains". Africans must realize that, most countries of the world only need their resources but not their partnership. The difference is clear, and every Africans with eyes could understand this when carefully turns open African institutional and political history. Men history may not have been turned-apart by his ineffectiveness nor have his visions, yet, the messages of his discovery last to pave ways for his posterity. The African had suffered from a dictatorship of human souls by humans who are regarded as Africans Messiah. A shame for the indifference (Shaibu, 6th, 2014) as we have seen in the past expression, maybe African transitions to the democratization as a Western solution to Africans may have lost its track record but how could this view be explained? The next section delves into these challenges.

Stages twenty-three

Democratizing an investment in the Africa?

'Analyzing the Chinese strategic partnership into African countries'

'The Chinese Opportunity and the global drama'

Interest and politics have lavish scores for political dichotomy in the African continent over the past decade, but the difference is that the contemporary African states may have turned out another cold war's in chores of African states between the emerging so called super powers and the elsewhere formal colonial super powers. This situation may have propelled us to understand the different changes in the geopolitical mechanization changing face in Africa state for a different purpose and involvement. For example, one Chinese expert beliefs that the 'China view on Africa increases as quote 'Whatever change may occur in the universe, our friendship with Africa will not change, our commitment to deepening mutually beneficial cooperation and achieving common development with Africa will not change, and our policy of supporting Africa's economic and social development will not change'. So far... in which ever ways may look at this ideology, the reality is 'African states are less captured as dumping the ground for the every emerging power in the global politics, but with a less curing design for the Africans needs and industrial development. Has Chinese emerging democratizing African states through huge investment change any extraordinary live hood? Maybe Yes or No. only Africans can tell what actually in going deep in the fabrics of their continent's political economy. To underpin the Chinese partnership in the African continent, we must acknowledge that, the Chinese see Africa only from the resources lens, aerial greens land, energy environment as well as cheap law position respectively as the key for their foreign policy project in Africa. When we talk of Chinese in Africa, we must recognize that in every yen spent in Africa, it is provided by the Chinese domestic strategic partnership policy towards Africa. We for instance, we acknowledge that its only a mathematic profession we could find a universal language as one plus one equals to two then; we must realize that, they are nothing like universal democracy which all nations should be subjected to the same policies. This is because of different greed are quite opposite in but erasing the completion as neither in decision making nor policy formulations. The Chinese scenario offers another alternative way to think about our politics towards Africa as neither strategic partner nor comrade. This helps explain a diametric global shift in moral reasoning and political thinking about democracy and what is not democratic. However, It was from this several assumptions that the Chinese had to empower its strategic investment directly into the African continent, while doing everything achievable to topple and further break-down the international stiffness to the African countries. On the other hand, profit –seeking strategies is certainly the Chinese policy towards Africa by gearing huge investment into the continent as well as undermining the Western strategic influence in Africa as we could observe from the current Chinese towering commitment to partnership with Africans without preserving selectivity. Nevertheless, what kind of long term challenges faces African states cooperation in dealings with the Chinese at the ends of the 21st century? While in own observations from the political, psychological point of view, the key problem of human ageing civilization is that, there has been a Constance negligence to understand the changes taking place within our environments and the universe, and this lack of knowledge had to pencil the entire Western visions to continue dancing to the song of their past even when the music had been stopped nor suspended long ago by globalizations. Thus, who, consequently, could re-discover this lost human inadequacy and failures to recognize when it is over?" Shaibu, 2014) In the final analyzes with reference to the Chinese policy towards Africa continent, we should over estimate the consequence of the Chinese domestic challenges back in Asians sub-regions. Yet, there may have reached a profound period beyond manageable and the simple solutions is to look down to Africa for survival while the impact would largely be left over for the Africa states when its over, the African people had no common ideas about what the Chinese interest with their massive investment in African nations stands for, but the posterity of African's generation will definitely understand and change the needed amendments. This is because the current African leaders had no single clue about the pistol behind them. Even so, While the international super powers are being locked in contention over African resources, the problems still remain that who is actually playing the perfect game to save Africans from the dependency? In whichever way, whether the Chinese will constantly stand by Africans after the period of the current desperate huge investments in African is yet to be ascertained. Although, it is mine believed that super powers may have adjusted their global strategic towards Africa. Let us be aware that Africa stood on the wrong stages of great ambitions for its resources more than that of the demands for partnership.

Stages twenty-four

'Is African's Nations Actually Failing in the 21st Century'?
The Fall of Great Ambitions in Africa

For several decades and half, especially between the 60s and towards the ends of the 20th centuries, the elsewhere colonizers of the African continents had to re-design their strategic narratives to re-occupied their formal colonial safe heavens for their own strategic ambitions irrespective of how such their demands may hurt the struggle societies to escape their past captivity. This scene had to emphasize the ever increasing dangers being posted out by external fabrics foiling the African failing from sustaining their pan Africanism struggle of the 60s. However, to dealt with such problems, many questions on building relations on how to reach out to foreign countries, specifically to the Western countries for collaborations settling the African environmental tensions, especially those created in the period of colonization before the 60s. Although, after a decade of precious without in rebuilding the protected states in Africa without anything tangible to show for it, the recent emerging era of Chinese's in Africa had to uproot other dimensions towards how the Western powers have placed African in their domestic foreign policy. In contrast, their practical reasons to reflect that majority of tactics towards Africans is to gain ground about controlling their resources by whatsoever it may cost as the West may not longer want to afford to lose control of its mission already established. Even when the number of failing states had increases in African states, little is being told about a sound strategic policy towards the underlying dynamism in the African sub-regions. Nevertheless, the global focus is being positioned on the importance of Africa in the most Western foreign policy, but what roles could be the beneficiary for the African people at the long-distance posterity is what the majority of Africans had never been told by both the West nor the emerging super powers in Africa from Chinese to Brazil, India and the elsewhere Russians demanding African's relations. But one of the interesting things I know about the Africans stages of civilization and re-colonization is that, underdevelopment in Africa continent continued to be one of the key factor's by which the majority of African leaders' hardly forecast, there have potentially inability to identify with where to initiate ideas in resolving their own predicaments in Africans ways. And I think one of the radical places to start is for Africans to have a re-think about proper-integration procedure **(PIP)** that unless such decisions are designed to harmonize, the way's Africans see themselves not separate but one continent and people, Africa's people escaping their captivity will press on to last as long as history continues to be told until time indefinite. Perhaps, as many of us could notice today, the balance of global has changed completely and it seems to me that most Western countries are not in fully aware of this natural phenomenon. Indeed, this situation will further indicate that the emerging struggles to balance the disappearing hegemony on its highest level of tensions and diplomacy in the 21st century towards most African countries. Therefore, to understand this fresh predicament, we must look afresh how we see the changes within our minds. It furthers means the courses of human history have not been fully settled only in the values of the Western civilizations. This series of journey had continued from the past according to the legacy of human destiny beyond what we have been told by the Western values. For instance, African continents had delivered a significant contribution to the Western civilizations, although, many of such contribution were left without further recognition beyond their existence in the past, and we could acknowledge these fabric isolations through the Europeans view about Africa before the transitions to slave trading commences. An English traveler who visited Abyssinia in the 19th century declared the Gada system of democracy superior to all existing republican systems of government in the world. (W. Plowden, Travels in Abyssinia,1868). Also, Johns Hopkins, observed: "The Ombudsman seems to be an African invention, even if better known in the West by a Scandinavian name." ("Changes in the New Order and the Place for the Old", in Zartman, 2000). Perhaps, I think one of the radical places to start is for Africans to accept a re-think about PIP that unless such decisions are being designed to harmonize, the way's Africans see themselves not separate but one continent and people, Africa's people escaping their captivity will press on to last as long as history continues to be told until time indefinite. Perhaps, as many of us could notice today, the proportion of global power has changed completely, and it seems to me that most Western nations are not in fully aware of this natural phenomenon. Indeed, this situation will add an extra indication that the emerging struggles to balance the disappearing hegemony on its highest level of tensions and diplomacy in the 21st century towards most African countries. Therefore, to understand this fresh predicament, we must look afresh how we interpret the changes within our minds. It furthers means the courses of human history have not been fully settled only in the values of the Western civilizations. This series of journey had continued from the past according to the legacy of human destiny beyond what we have been told by the Western values than that of Europe. For instance, African continents had delivered a significant contribution to the Western civilizations, although, many of such contribution were left without further recognition beyond their existence in the past, and we could acknowledge these fabric isolations through the Europeans view about Africa before the transitions to slave trading commences. An English traveler who visited Abyssinia in the 19th century declared the Gada system of democracy superior to all existing republican systems of government in the world. (W. Plowden, Travels in Abyssinia, 1868). Furthermore, Johns Hopkins, observed: "The Ombudsman seems to be an African invention, even if better known in the West by a Scandinavian name" ("Changes in the New Order and the Place for the Old," in Zartman, 2000). If we must account that Africans are in the states of collapse, we should also be quick to identify with the factors responsible for the Africans failures. This is because, before the issue of slave trading and other inconvenience generated from the external force which invaded the Africans cultures, privacy of the strangers from oversea; the Africa's had established unquestionable civilized institutions, which had flourished over 3, 000 years ago before the contacts with the Europeans under which later leads to the current changes that have suspended the Africans history. While it is obvious, we recognize that most westerns hardly will deny the importance of African's cultures, traditions and arts in the various museums in the 21st century. However, the African had no culture or stable institutions, and it is only the worst that could settle Africans on the path to redemption. What does one do in such a scenario? While it is also important, we must, for that most Africans intellectual had not fully recovered the impacts of the triangular trade, which leads to the exportations of Africans as cheap labour to the Western world which had in the 21st century help in neither contributing nor promoting the widening gap of European's economic developments. Also, as many had forgotten this inflections, many Africans have long ago shifted identify and to further reconstruct the converted instability established the unequal state's creation in African call sovereign countries today. Therefore, as far as civilization and underdevelopment are concerned, Africans. As a Henry Moore inscription of the inspiration, he drew from exhibits in the British Museum, now in the Museum of Mankind: I was particularly interested in the African and Pacific sculptures and felt that 'primitive' was a misleading description of them, suggesting crudeness and incompetence. It was obvious to me that these artists were not trying – and failing – to represent the human form naturalistically, but that they had definite traditions of their own From Henry Moore at the British Museum (British Museum Publications, 1981), p. 11. Undoubtedly, Since Europeans discovered 'African wealth, there have been at different times in human history, different kind of massages of diplomacy towards Africa and one thing often remain clear, Establishing every content of policy towards changing the patronage to African's adequate information on establishing African on industrial heaven had never form parts of the Western imagination despite long awaited needs of Africans on the fence of Europe seeking for the most changing relations which had freezing the entire Africans nations with poverty and industrial pollution by the Western companies. In my opinion, there is know any kind of dangerous imperialism than the one most Western country's designed to contain African wealth but without developing their wealth. The West, However, sees natural resources first before any aids and assistance are often calculated on the spirit, on what is gained in return for their national interest. Maybe this may quickly be the open eyes of Chinese in Africa to challenge the West in Africa again for the second time. Nevertheless, what is the difference between a leopard and Tiger? Both are dangerous animal that you cannot allow them to live under one roof with your domestic animals. How should Africans see their own future posterity being from one generation to another place under constant dependency with all their resources? The most interesting game plans are the West re-designs tactics of self help in African continents, buying every greener space, lands in Africa for the European cultivation of food production for exportations from African to Europe. Do not forget, African trade with the West keeps suffering from rejection by the West. This is because the West is in tight control to see Africans as dependent on the Western ends well only. Who can change this scenario in 'Not' by Africans themselves? It is a pity. My pen is running out of ink and all together in Africa continent. We have all the available resources to produce any kind of gold pens demand by me, but discuss we do not have the technology. I needed to contact my friends in the West to get me some pen to write. This has to be the way of Africa turned to the centre for wasteful product in Europe. While many evidences from the historical fact have to signal African advancement since post democratic transitions in Africa, the truth of the key facts about African states has been smuggled out from the African peoples' knowledge by the black men imperialist who are today in collaboration to destroy African's stages of civilization. We could see why every ambition to celebrate Africa among wealthy continents like Asia, Russia, American, Europeans could not work out in Africa. At most, several Europeans nations are visa free to members of their integration partners, whereas in Africa, every effort by Africans to stand up to this practical unification which could set Africans on the path to survival and sustainable control of their own destiny in harmony had to be disorganized lobbed out by groups of unknown Western magnets. I am suggesting that as long as African keeps betraying their continents, states, nations for their self-aggrandizement, at some points if care is not taken African history will be deleted by wars, violence, terrorism or even explored by dangerous weapons donated by the Western comrade to safeguard African security challenges as so called for their domestic needs while Africans will constantly remain frosting empire with wars and instability. Times to re-think beyond self, regions and groups in Africa continent but to work together as the people of one race and society (Shaibu, 5th, 2014)

Stages twenty-five

The Prophesy Behind Africa Predicaments
21st Century Re-birth of Africa in Global Debt Struck by Underdevelopment

> *"In observing himself, a man notices that self-observation itself brings about certain changes in the inner process. He begins to understand that self-observation is an instrument of self-change, a means of awakening"* [40]

This study will argue that the emerging neo-imperialism in Africa continent by the so called '***emerging powers in the global politics*** 'may not be the shaping eagles of what actually defines Africa debates as several scholars would want us to acknowledge nor subjecting majority of African leaders alone being under a special hard-core of their countries failures, but the fabricated ideas to caged Africans through multi-national borrows to Africans are the major burdens defining Africans states into inability to facilitates the continent of Africa from securing liberty, development and security for the African citizens (Shaibu, 2014). This extended idea of colonialism has to be designed as one strong meaning that helps

---

[40] –(G.I. Gurfjieff) See, Elina St-onge, (2014) pp.104 , to change the world, if we all took a moment to simply observe the world as it is, the evolution of our species would happen overnight.

to shape what Africans should be recognized in the international politics. Instance of Africa state's inability to sustain itself from dependency and corrupt practices may have strong links with this constructed ideology towards African states. Thoughtfully, the debt burden by its magnet designers and its servicing by the African collaborated leadership keep dates with ever increasing burden of aids nor call them scientific contribution in Africans had to in such a short period of time been flown into Europeans banks for safe keeping by its collaborators. I often recalled an adage in my private observation of our societies anarchy and instability and further note that *"do not always rush into mourning until you know or rather been told the truth. Its often belief in Africa that the truths rule the society of people (Shaibu, 21-09-2011)* I would want all of us to recognize that the debt burdens to Africa and the continuation of these design debts serving had in most of its cruel nature have to undermine in depth needs of the people of Africa to develop growths to the continent of African to its people and societies while often wearing the continent into an un-ending underdevelopment and backwardness. Once we both recognize the above perceptions of what made Africa a state of dependency, and then...We could know why Africa to my own intellectual uniqueness still believes that the Western continent had not intended to ever allow Africans to develop beyond dependency on their graphics ideas and strategies since emergency post-colonialism which started in the 50s. This has been how the statistic of failures befalling Africans states which in most occasions has a strong link to external collaborators, which had helped to invite the entire Africans states into chaotic, violent, negatives media coverage's to Africa. Then, how can Africans states be prominent above that of normal human liberty as defined by natural laws. Sometimes, many people wonder why has Africans people and society had to suffer too much of what had become like international collaboration to pencil African states into dependency. For example, The corrupt practices in Africa is not only the key factors that sustain several states into its states of being coined as 'frontier states' but those who enjoy providing the safe haven for those looting wealth's of Africans states are the main African problems. Thus, who has the consciences among several external forces in Africa to reduce their interest in Africa by practicing what is actually the modern moral integrity of liberty in the so call democratic principles towards Africa or to Africans people? Yes, the enormous wealth of Africa states, yet, in the hands of detrimental agony today is well designed under accomplishments of people who do not believe in seeing Africans free. In most painful remembering of the pan Africanize legacy, I often cry in confusion of what Africans at most thinks of themselves from the international perspectives. Although, I belief it to be correct that, this SO CALLED Africans problems have often been misinterpreted by focusing mainly on the Africans corrupt leaders forgetting that the links and the bridges that secures these laborious burdens to Africans are those constructed horizontally and possibly vertically with the clubs of external agency which we all know them today within you and I today. For instance, whenever, I would thought over Africa undemocratic states of frog's civilization, I think as regards also that Africa must be ready to secure its self release of the external hand-cuts through rejections of donated warning and policies to Africans states. Though, I often think again first thing about what the majority of those behinds African states may feel about the Africans people and states was to loan Africans money through aids cruelty, which may likely in many ways place Africans under the remote controls of those who develop this new imperialism. They have come to understand be inform or told of Africa extra multi-languages, cultures and projects in African continents as those with different with names there could use only to help secure to themselves not Africans the beauty of their policies as donors behind Africans people. Who is actually fooling each other in Africa? In turn, most Africans had turned to debt ridding nations as frontier states with the burden of debt serving with material wealth which is supposed to be used in securing Africans state stability and freedom of human existence. Let us not forget that this chronic links by most external forces and collaborators had shades Africans the liberty to understand the real facets of their key problems. Who is really against Africans development, security, underdevelopment and instability? And who has actually brought any problems in Africa states into peaceful conclusions without making a fortune from such engagements in Africa? For examples, Congo, Mali, Niger,

Cameroon etc. Nevertheless, most states in Africa have to be negatively been relegated as regrettable and the frontier states, as several states turn to anarchy over dependency on foreign aids through collaborations with multi-national magnets as joint policy advisers for Africans. This has been the implications for both Africans states from Ghana to Nigeria, sub-Sahara Africans etc. Perhaps, it will not be hard for anyone with intellectual sight to acknowledge that the entire Africa states had been position by those externally connection with both multi-nationals, Western banks nationally, IMF, World bank, etc. Through the prophecy of propagandas and procrastinations to secure their interest from the same frontier states despites the fact that such policies and design practices had death implications for Africans populations. Why should Africans states being torn into procrastination by donating Western ideas and policy that had no benefits to Africans people, society and continents? The real emerging collapse of Africa could at most recognize from (a) the debt serving scenario in collaboration with those who benefits from the amount of gains it accrue for the those agents (b) internationally design links who had protected Africans looted wealth into fully democratic states, though, what make them full democracies if they secure wealth of other nations in their counties to build their democracies (c) how true is the ever increasing aids, debts to Africans, contributions to helping Africans stability through gun purchase from our companies secure Africans peace?

I have for so stretched in acknowledging that people tend to come out for assistances specifically anything that could at the ends satisfy their needs without acknowledging the grave implications for their actions. *As Fanon puts it: Colonization is the organization of the domination of a nation after military conquest*[41] Are we today living in a world without moral conscience? What then defines the term democracy without moral conscience if people liberty and freedoms are not considered in our quest to amaze the entire world nor Africans under our control? The world is in the modern times, leaving under a severe hardship designs by man made by the you and me of the power and finances to purchase the world. Do we actually think of the nearest posterity implications' to our next generations? So many evils actions we both acted to push reduce several citizens of this great world into pre-matured deaths. How does this situation fit us if our own beloved citizens, children's and country's men are being locked up in such a dangerous acts of inhumanity to other nations? This event has been some of the strategic interest in Africa, which has helped to post-pond Africans liberty, development and freedom through individually cruelty against our people of different races. Now, after several years of our enduring contribution of Africans, the waves of stability have not been safe for Peace in Africa nor neither makes our products of weapons to Africans helps in establishing democratic stability as often insinuated for Africa

---

[41]   **Fanon, Frantz**, Towards the African Revolution (New York: Grove Press, 1967). Reprint of Pour la revolution Africana, Paris, 1964

freedom, instability, violence and captivity. We may even say, the principle use to fine turn Africans leaders is to procrastinate that Africans are making progress in the faces of anarchy, underdevelopment, poverty, insecurity and misery in Africa. In my view, no adequate knowledge about what is expected to initiate for its progression, stability, re-organization could ever come to the mind of those external networks of bodies of continent scrambling for the Africans today. I often emphasize their collaborative motives as those fashions under a canopy of self-aggrandizement. New forms of civilizations being calculated at the ends of post colonial and post 20th century to drive Africans from their genius determinations to changing the reflections of the African circumstances and to further improve recognitions of their inadequacies tricking the continents into misery. The massages of the Africans predicament are very clear today as wealthy and abundant green continents. Yet, who could establish this record straight as it reflects in meaning to 'who is actually saving another in the ways we both understood the global politics, dynamism and diplomacies in the 21st century? Still, we kept turning blind eyes to initiate what is right to say, but rather choose the negatives to disprove Africans stages of civilization. The begging question now beyond the cold war's already going on in African continents is that' how more long years should such cruelty of lack of interest in the Africa peoples, society and stability, development, liberty and recognitions in the international politics be expelled from the morally ways of policies towards African people and societies. Africans had already known about the procrastinations and further propaganda ideologies deploy by several forces in African continents. Even so, neither the Western mega multi-nationals understood the relevance's of acrimonious impact behinds each of them on the African continents. Media all recognition Africans states are frontiers states, this is not propaganda, but why is Africa in this shape?. The ongoing agenda of our various harmful techniques and unjust policies making African look like a body of stagnant continents helps to establish the constant preaching we all designs in Africa today. I strongly hold truth to say that No one thinks the rights of most African people and we must learn to accept them as equal as we all are being made as the same Africans societies. I will argue that any idea of democracy to the African nation states which does not recognize equal treatment of Africans in both trade, businesses, technology sharing, for getting ideas of technical borrowing through aids, which I found out as equally important in the states of nature, it should be discarded. Thus, if enforced to African without Africans demands by the majority of African citizens, then we should acknowledge those ideas, design purposefully to dethrone the entire Africans traditions, liberty, sovereignty etc. A term mechanically calculated to reject the Africans values, identity of the African societies and races for the benefits of artificially diabolical self-aggrandizement of some members of another powerful but weak continent (Shaibu, Feb. 7th, 2014) its therefore, possible we reflects that nothing fundamentally are important for those mega evil-gangsters interest of being equal to replicate equal partnership with Africans. But we often see in Africa are such radical re-design of formal imperial networks that is so dangerous to the detriments of what Africans are today. This ideas, However, are very much running out fresh in the veins of those who do not beliefs in seeing African continent secure themselves a permanent released from external captivity so that they could initiate ideas of their cultural heritage to sustained their pan Africans legacies in rebuilding their own traditional values to their people, societies and continent. I am very much confident that '*THERE IS NO PLANET NOR SUN THAT COULD STOPS ONE TO STAND STILL IF YOU DO NOT SO AGREED TO ANY FORM OF ENFORCES FALANCY WITHIN WHERE YOU CERTAINTLY STAND. IF YOU KNOW EXACTLY WHO YOU ARE, AND YOUR PURPOSE WELL UNDERSTOOD. NOTHING STOPS THE FLOW OF REALITY AND DESTINY (Shaibu, 8 April 2014) Africans must search for their own destiny in this era. A journey expected of them long before colonialism.*

Stages twenty-six

Is Africa Encircled by Procrastination?

The 21st Century Inquiry into Africa Obstacles'

Why it is always Africa?

"I have never been able to conceive how any rational being could propose happiness to himself from the existence of power over others in the face of their poverty, destitution and misery" (Thomas Jrfferson,1792-1826, Shaibu,2014)

The states of various African sovereign nations are in miserable designs by doctrines of our actions in both past and in the contemporary world politics. Still, how does this situation affects our rational, moral, democratic idealism in the 21st century? Evidently, several increasing global effort to smuggle African continents into their foreign and domestic politics. This situation had to signal other meanings of calls to states in Africa and the people to be wondering about what is actually tripping the entire global powers into chasing for the continent they have often rejected as frontiers, war zone, no go area, terrorist haven etc. What had eventually changed that makes Africans so important in the 21st century? I first answer to strike straight to the meanings of 1929 depression into the Western capitalism idealism. A specific failure that leads all through to several wars in Europe down to around 1939 etc. The West is solvent no doubt the capitalism idealism has already reached the state of confusion and decays beyond what the media often underline to secure Africa continents as their rescue domestically. However, why has Africans never seems to be recognized as a surviving template for the Western insufficiency? There are several instances I would be glad to mention here, but due to time measurement, maybe we could talk about few countries in debt where without Africa, many of them will be like another Congo. Which means states of violence and wars etc.? For examples, ***at least today*** in the 21st century, (14 14 African Countries) had been neither design nor packages since their independence around 1961 by France to Pay Colonial Tax for the Benefits of Slavery and Colonization which these countries in Africa despite their peoples misery, poverty, underdevelopment and further unemployment are still feeding the French government[42]. While the West and the press in the Francis keep blaming Africa for poverty, instability and underdevelopment. Their various political messages around Africa, which several journalists in most Western country are not being informed by their government and in the cause of their engagement with their various professions. I begged the questions that why several internal crises in sovereign nations in African become the so call political races for most Western countries to get involves. Even as we speak, over 85% of about thirteen (13) African countries are said to be the key duties of the French government of this powerful country in Africa deposit their foreign reserve into the France central bank under French minister of Finance as the chief accountant. This is absolutely unbelievable and questions in the 21st century, No wonder French sees Africa as its destine reality to remain struggle

---

[42] **Mawuna Remarque KOUTONIN,**(Tuesday, January 28th, 2014)
http://www.siliconafrica.com/france-colonial-tax/

to keep holding tight to them despite several calls against the French government to rest sovereign nations in Africa. It is now clear to all. But, how longer MORE?

Take a look at this map in Africa about the French government holding tight to poor country in a quest to smashing their resources while downgrading the society's citizens into poverty and underdevelopment. This is a serious political suicide and this country already had no further for their citizens seeing the light of liberty everyone is dreaming of becomes.

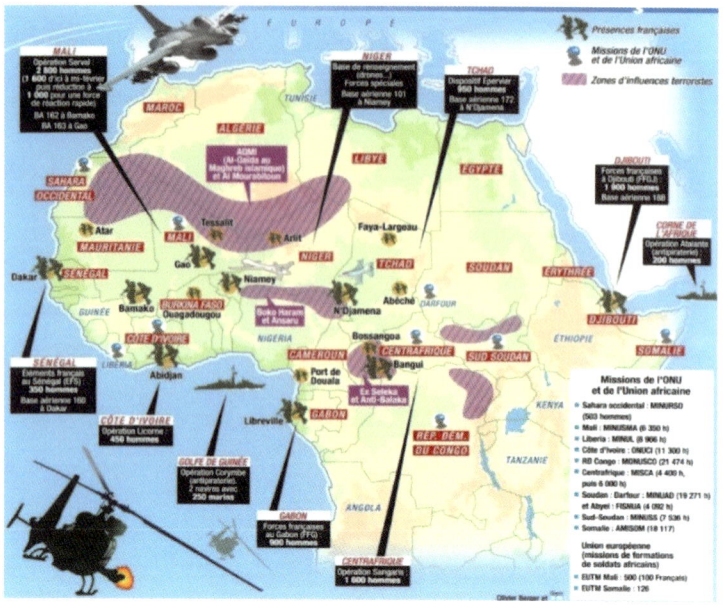

Perhaps, many nations may have given their consent about African people, society and generation without the notice of African people that 'Africans can never survive as stable continent. How did we come to this conclusion? Its pertinent we recognize that until a man has given up his dreams, No man, nations, continents and society, no matter how powerful could expelled other peoples and their nations dreams to be developed beyond dependency on foreign. Even when the entire world has seemed to be embezzled by wars of interest against societies, poverty and misery, many of us refuse to accept that this century is quite different from those we had all wittiness behind us today. Indeed, While several countries, continent expresses their calculated demands to control others through forces, diplomacy, tactics and deceptions, the scholars who are prominent researchers should be objectives in their scholars' research work instead of being diverted their studies into the favouring interest of their popular governments against the competent willingness of the people of different races in their own society and continent. Even as I write this book, many journalists and interest lobbies had established their cruelties networks in Africa which had to potentially help in pulling out false claims about African continents and society into a global arena. Thus, as we call struggle to publish what happens in Africa, especially those negative once, which often quickly focus on how Africa had a damaging ratio of underdevelopment caused by Africans own leaders in their society, if we are most dear to follow a similar journalism with objectivity about Africa continents, we will be able to understand by now where most African problems are being designed. We all know the games and several African youth remember why and the reasons for their most predicament about their chartered dreams. Who owns tomorrow in the global politics? This questions should be answers within us.

Stages seven

The Fragile States in Africa:

Aid for Africa Civilization
What Next After Aids, Democratization into Africa?

(No country will entirely exist while still setting on the gun-power of its historical colonial traps called sovereign nations around Africa. We must learn to reflect meaning

for our existence. When we understand this point, then we can now feel confident to initiate our own national guards of our citizen's liberty, freedom from oppression and racial discriminations. Only when this healthy ground is wet, we can pull out our traditional bans to plan our seeds as nation, countries where African liberty will be secured (Shaibu, 30. 03.2013)

Only one equitable solution in Africa today I really think worth an African imagination at some point towards the continent re-positioning in the 21st century. And even if there are many, the one captured in the above quotes signifies the entire dreams of African people, solution that could force to establish the well being of African integration and further could sanction several Africans into the unbelievable task of releasing the African society from committing a continental suicide through un-ending exploitations from the continent of Africa. I have noticed since 1994 trade agreements between Africa and the West as one beginning of fractional designs to seize the African position from the global recognition but being it whatsoever, the destiny of African people, resources and society is such a phenomenon that is beyond any gurus to comprehend and much as this situation keep upgrading from one level to another and the rate of globalization of African knowledge in the field of science, technology, economic, politics, diplomacy, tactics and game theory. I foresee Africans miss-leading the cooperate magnet behind African liberation into a sinking disaster in as much as I could feel it before the end of the

21st century (Shaibu, 2014) this is an Africa era, we both neither agree or disagree to perish but nothing will ever change the cause of African society being elevated beyond the states called frontiers and fragile today. First of all, I often suggest to Africans, have we really found out why Africans are not cooperating with each other? Perhaps, nothing disintegrate people like deceptions and Africa people must learn to understand that, there are several networks already been perfected historically to contain Africa at post-colonialism and this network had to my own understanding comes to an ends in the 21st century. No doubt, Africans must quickly form an imaginary session to re-organize the breathing of African people, society and continents. And this view, I will suggest, it is not a matter of being help that building constructed with signal to China about anything African discuss in the so called AU house neither constructed nor rather donated by the Chinese's government in Addis- Abba. Africa holds key to essential particles of international laws and if their positions must be meaning and logical to define their own continent, there must recognize to secure their own freedom domestically first both small states and big state in Africa must set on one negotiating table to drink cola together according to African traditions where no betrayal ever exist from this forum. The pretext that international laws had limits Africans from taking their traditional homeland from the radical quest for exploitation that had to cake Africa with the arbitrary hammer and nail is obviously questionable and Africa should reject these claims to re-organize their society in the most effective and transparent manner possible. It has been quite regrettable that African sees wealth accumulations first before their own people's liberty and freedom under, which gave the external forces an embracing shadow to encircle the continent from every angle of the earth they felt possible. Indeed, even the Bible recognizes that vanity is vanity, but for the sake of our unknown tomorrow, we must value our own brothers and sister so that our days on earth will be recognized on the last day. This view had to supersede that of most African thinking about building an empire on earth at the cost of their society and people being design to be a terrorist and rebel pursue to in maturing death through their poverty and under privilege. There has been radical opportunity taking by the most external agencies in Africa through a calculated politically method to favours some African leaders interestedly to place Africans into a permanent stagnation and poverty. Although, out of fifty-four African fragile cottages of the Western world called sovereign state hardly been recognized by the same forces that design what each nation and leaders get from each country that tend to smuggled Africans into their private door-post while many Africans leaders are still sleeping in their luxury of favourism. Yet, I am not writing this book to interpret any procrastination about Africa by the Western media nor anybody who might find this book aggressive, but I try to build it from my own intellectual knowledge about what is actually happening to African people and society to help the posterity of Africans see and follow to understand what is specifically standing against their own free will, liberty and natural freedom. Even when we all being told nor recognizes we are all born free, but in Africa, most of us with black skins are often recognized as third citizens. Who defines this agenda is one damaging instrument ever done to human creation which does not touch only Africans people and society but to the entire world races. The write of a knowledge which I well understood is that your own destiny is defined by your contribution to making a society better and at most a peaceful society. Beyond this divine which design to say, I fear no false accusations against the will of my destine opportunity to be born and preach the right and wrong of what I fully understood by African people stages of poverty and destitutions and no regression after being tendered to Africans for the painful industrial acrimony package for their society and people over the last decade which had to continue until the date. The history of our actions defines how the world will be shaped in the future. In my view also, African people are now fully aware about several tactics design to mandating Africans into constant exploitations through some mechanical policies and advisers which had to help disintegrate the entire African society over the last decade. For instance, the European Union had objected diplomatically to form a round table with the AU on several occasions owing to its idealism in the Africa as mandated by its policy advisers but rather chooses to comradeship with an individual head of state and government of Africans of their interest on the matters that affect the two continents. At most,

European Union failed to realize the significance of African population, which could in the real sense of the point could be divided into three of the entire Europe today. What is wrong with their decision to form this type of acrobatic decisions? It is simply to deny African occasion to integrate that could further help them to cement their position together in the international politics. We the Africans had continued to follow this mechanism without interest rather to say, but to see what those African leaders selected should achieve for Africa over the past decade. Much indeed, the story is often the same, preaching the gospel of political strategies to development in Africa through aids etc. That is all. Africa is a fragile state... Why not? While about 16 billion Euros had at some points within this century were flown to some Africans leaders entitle as gift to purchase luxury and benefiting cars as the Western collaborators. Today, we find AU is also being encircled in the European logo in partnership with Africa, which in other ways, meaning an agenda to contain the entire Africa as the shadow indicates. This is because it has been said Africans had no knowledge to read and interprets any fabricated terms to Africans over the last decade.

So for, what about the issue of today with relation to the 21st century Africa continent in our hand's? If we still think about the historical past of Africans today, we are actually making grave mistakes about Africans people. Except if Africans who do not care to know about nothing happening, but Africans are fully unique with exceeding knowledge of unthinkable in the 21st century. No doubt, an experience with an African determines intellect will tell you beyond your comprehension. Yet, Africans allow themselves to be subjected to the third class scenario. Why this dichotomy? It is only a pity Africans had to come this long before realizing the occasion that had pencil them down into incomprehensible misery by date. But what can we say of the 21st century of Africa determination to over-turn this nemesis that had to canopy Africans into frontier states? For example, since 2005 specifically in Africa, only one small African country Eritrea government was able to successfully beyond expectation of internationally condemned to secure the Eritreans from the hands of internationally calculated financial aid magnet by the West against their society, states and people. Perhaps, all their devotion in running their own country was based on self help in rebuilding their cottage empire, which was indirectly constructed by the empire builder Italian around 1939. They stood their system of traditional African society structure of democracy as country by advancing their countries needs without functioning with any form of financial capitalist aids shadow in what I often terms as ' *evil spirit spell into Africa'*. As we speak, this small country is perfect doing well. Other examples, how many countries in Africa who received this' evil spirit spell into Africa as Aid' ever done any tangible things that reflects the so called billions given to Africans states? Which country can adequately give account about how this money being spent now allowed reproducing divided into those states? No single country in Africa could justify the position of these questions. Still, where is the so called aid money in Africa? Are we actually being told specifically in Africa how the aid stuff ended up as several Western media wants us to admit?. No. Indeed, billions of every Euro in Africa for aids, within the next 15 minutes of its landing in Africa found its steps back into Western national banks, Swiss banks, and into unknown property purchase in various European continent and country and no country in the West can claim not guilty of this suicidal fraud to African states and the people. We must make sense of our contribution to Africa nor forget it all together. It is painful to send simply a drug to heal stomach pains into Africa instead of building the same company that help secure the entire generation of civilizations in Africa by this company. I specifically see every entire final product to Africans as a means for public propaganda which is baseless about how the West is helping the Africa continent. However, What I did know is that Africans leaders received aids finances with a big hulk on their throat to return them back to base as a channel properly design to secure a linkage for the entire African corrupt leaders with the Western collaborators. Africa as fragile state is a mere propaganda design by those who very much and fully aware of the actions betraying Africans sustainability (Shaibu, 9.4.2014)

Stages twenty-eight

Conclusions

Ultimately, these era is an African hope and destiny to rule the world. Thus, A mission if carefully taking that could secure Africans elevation beyond being used and neglect. Therefore, All the regrettable record of Africans with regards to their historical past slave trades, colonization, scrambles and the contemporary invisible new imperialism should be an excuses for Africans not resist the future or a continuity of such evil past but it should serve as one single lessons in their hearts that should be well understood and further endure in the hearts of African youths. In order that, appropriate theory could be invented by Africans youths to fight for their eradication. Remove the bases of the misery cause by past. if it means one day, that Africans should be free from captivity. Without doubt, Africans must secure and further sustain this era which belongs to Africa advanced beyond the indebted acrobatic fabrication on their doorsteps..

Book of facts; & References

Shaibu, Danladi. Sunday (2012) The Memory of Berlin Conference 1884-1885; "African Questions "What matters in the 21st century? A report delivered at the international conference of Young scholars. And subsequently form part of my intellectual book on (Who is against the Nigeria Democracy, pp. 55-67 . 21st march 2014-04-07 (ISBN-978-3-659-17116-1)

Amin, S. (1972): 'Underdevelopment and Dependence in Black Africa - Origins
. And 525.

Basil Davidson, the African past, chronicles from Antiquity to the modern times. PENGIUM ,IBRARY. 1966, PP 17-33.

See A. Bolaji Akinyemi, Conflict of interest in Africa; The OAU and the Concept of Non-Interference in Internal Affairs of Member States, 46 Brit. Y.B. Int'l L. 393 (1972-73) (discussing how the effectiveness of the OAU could be improved if the OAU stops hiding behind the non-interference clause of Article III (2)); Obi Okongwu, The OAU Charter and the Principles of Domestic Jurisdiction in Intra-African Affairs, 13 Indian J. Int'l L. 589 (1973).

See, Jeffery Herbst. (1996-97) responding to state failures in Africa, International Security, Vol. 21, no 3, winter 1996-7. pp. 175-183

Clapham, Christopher S. 1996, Fragile state and international organization. African and the international system; the politics of state's survival. pp. 1014, African foreign Affairs 1960s

Ralph Folsom, the European Union; Part One, July 25th 2012. University of San Diego School of Law
See Aristide Briand, the 1925 the French Minister of Foreign Affairs, said at the occasion of the Locarno Pact (Locarno is a small township along the Italian sea, where a peace pact has been ratified): "In Locarno we spoke European, this is a new language, which has now to be taken".

James G. March & Johan P. Olsen, AU Act, supra note 14, art. 4 (m). See generally James G. March & Johan P. Olsen, Democratic Governance (1995) (describing an agenda of how individuals and societies can achieve institutions that make politics civil and capable).

Daniel Bach, (1986). "France's involvement in sub-saharan Africa" in Amadu Sesay Ed, Africa and Europe: from partition to Interdependence or dependence?
Shaibu, D. S, On African foreign policy. Edited by Martin Riegl, Jakub Landovsky) **Strategic and Geopolitical Issues in the**

Contemporary World, Hardcover – July 1, 2013

Jean Monnet: Memoirs, London 1976, p. 323. See also, *Further information: www.coe.int, on the treaties and conventions of the Council of Europe:*
http://conventions.coe.int, on the European Court of Human Rights: www.echr.coe.int .

Paul Williams (2004). "Britain and Africa after the Cold war: beyond damage limitation?" in Taylor
and Williams Africa in International Politics

M. Mbuh. (2004) International Law and Conflicts: Resolving Border and Sovereignty Disputes in Africa. I Universe, Inc.460 pages,
Lord Salisbury, in "Bakassi who has Bakassi?" (West Africa 18-24 April 1994) (ISBN: 0595297072
See, Issues on Eyptian revolutions;
http://www.presstv.ir/detail/2013/12/02/337855/african-genocide-pretext-for-french-plunder/

Egypt Must Reach an Agreement with IMF, Kerry Says;
http://www.presstv.ir/detail/2013/03/02/291626/egypt-must-strike-deal-with-imf-kerry/

J.W. Smith, Economic Democracy; The Political Struggle for the 21st Century, (M.E. Sharpe, 2000), p.95

(Nelson   Gomonda,   2013).
http://www.vanguardngr.com/2013/03/334-million-people-in-sub-
sahara-africa-lack-access-to-clean-water-wateraid-
2/#disqus_thread'

Will Kymlicka & Magda Opalski, can liberal pluralism be exploited? Western political theory and ethnic relations in Eastern Europe, pp.227,

S. De Bogou; France plays dirty game in CAR:
http://www.presstv.ir/detail/2013/11/30/337501/france-cause-of-colonial-crisis-in-car/

Jackson, (1996) Ibid, pp. 10

Murrary Milgate & Shannon C. Stimson (2009) After Adam Smith A century of Transformation in Politics and political Economy., Princeton University press Oxford.

Myron Echenberg, (1857-1960) colonial conscripts, pp. 127-145. The Tirailleurs Senegalais in French. Social history of Africa. Series Editors; Allen Isaacman and Luise White,

Marth. L. Cottam. Dieth-Uhler. Elena, M. Thomas. P, (2010) An Introduction to political psychology, 2rd edition, pp324-327,

Basil Davidson, (1964) the African past, the chronical from Antiquity to the modern times. pp. 265-274

Ibid, 273

Clapham, C. 1996. Africa and the international system: the politics of state survival. Cambridge: Cambridge University Press.

Herbst, J. 1997. Responding to State Failure in Africa, in Michael Brown, Owen Cote, Sean Lynn-Jones and Steven Miller (Eds.), Nationalism and Ethnic Conflict Cambridge, Massachusetts: The MIT Press

Davidson, B. 1992. The black Man's Burden: Africa and the curse of the nation state. London: James Currey.

Baranyi S., and Powell, K., Fragile States, Gender Equality and Aid Effectiveness: A Review of Donor Perspectives, The North-South Institute

Rodrigo Bueno Lacy and Henk van Houtum (December 5, 2013) **Europe's Border Disorder** http://www.e-ir.info/2013/12/05/europes-border-disorder/

Martin J. Wiener *(2013)* **the** Idea of "Colonial Legacy" and the Historiography of Empire,

Journal of The Historical Society. Volume 13, Issue 1, pages 1–32, March 2013 *Ibid, 1*

JEHRON MUHAMMAD, **(JUN 30, 2009) is an Africa, throwing off the yoke of dependency?** http://www.finalcall.com/artman/publish/Perspectives_1/Is_Africa _throwing_off_the_yoke_of_dependency.shtml

LOUIS FARRAKHANN, (*DEC* 10, 2013) 'SEPARATION! Independence!

http://www.finalcall.com/artman/publish/Minister_Louis_F arrakhan_9/article_101034.shtml

Amin, S. (1972): 'Underdevelopment and Dependence in Black Africa - Origins and Contemporary Forms,' Journal of Modern African Studies 10, 4

(December): 503-525.

Markovitz, (1977: 25-97; **Shaw,** 1977b),Seminar on Non-capitalist Development in Africa in Helsinki in August 1976 and at the annual conference of the African Studies Association in Boston in November 1976.)

Carmody and Taylor, 2010, quote in Scoones, Lidia and H. Tugendhat 2013, IDS Bulletin Vol. 44, number 4, July 2013

New Development Encounters; China and Brazil in African Agriculture.

See, http://www.china.org.cn/world/2009-11/09/content_18849890.htm

Xinhua, (November 9, 2009) Full text of Wen's speech at 4th Ministerial Conference of FOCAChttp://www.china.org.cn/world/2009-11/09/content_18849890.htm

Dependence or Development: International and Internal Inequalities in Africa, *Development and Change, 8* (1977), 377408

166

Carmody and Taylor, 2010, quote in Scoones, Lidia and H. Tugendhat 2013, IDS Bulletin Vol. 44, number 4, July 2013 New Development Encounters; China and Brazil in African Agriculture. Contemporary Forms,' Journal of Modern African Studies 10, 4 (December): 503-525.

Welsh, Jennifer M. (2003), (Editor), *Humanitarian Intervention and International Relations*
Chapter 2 "Limiting Sovereignty", Chapter 5 "The United Nations and Humanitarian Intervention", Chapter 7 "Humanitarian Intervention and International Society: Lessons from Africa" [ONLINE - www.oxfordscholarship.com]

Tatiana Carayannis, (2003)'The Complex Wars of the Congo: Towards a New Analytic Approach,' Journal of Asian and African Studies 2003, 2-3: 232-255

http://jas.sagepub.com/cgi/content/abstract/38/2-3/232

Markovitz, 1977: 25-97; Shaw, 1977b). Seminar on Non-capitalist Development in Africa in Helsinki in August 1976 and at the annual conference of the African Studies Association in Boston in November 1976.

Thad Dunning, (2008). *Crude Democracy*, Cambridge University Press. Macartan Humphreys, Jeffrey Sachs, Joseph E. Stiglitz, 2007. *Escaping the Resource Curse.*
Columbia University Press.

Eghosa Osaghae, (1995), "The ogoni uprising, oil politics, minority agitation and the future of the Nigerian State" African Affairs 94 (1995), 325-344. [ONELINE VIA JSTOR

Geo-Jaja, M.A., Magnum, G. (2001). Structural adjustment as an inadvertent enemy of human development in Africa. *Journal of Black Studies* 32:30-49

Basil Davidson, *Black Star: A View of the Life and Times of Kwame Nkrumah (London: James Currey, 1973), 94.*

Nicholas van de Walle (1999) 'Aid's Crisis of Legitimacy: Current Proposals and Future Prospects' in African Affairs (98: 392) pp. 337-352 [ONLINE]

Fanon, Frantz, Towards the African Revolution (New York: Grove Press, 1967). Reprint of Pour la revolution Africaine, Paris, 1964

Dependence or Development: International and Internal Inequalities in Africa, *Development and Change, 8* (1977), 377408

–**(G.I. Gurfjieff) See, Elina St-onge,** (2014) pp.104 , to change the world, if we all took a moment to simply observe the world as it is, the evolution of our species would happen overnight.

See, http://www.china.org.cn/world/2009-11/09/content_18849890.htm

Full text of Wen's speech at 4th Ministerial Conference of FOCAC; Xinhua, November 9, 2009, http://www.china.org.cn/world/2009-11/09/content_18849890.htm

Half the Day Is Night (1994)   -
http://www.locusmag.com/1999/Issues/10/McHugh.html

Mawuna Remarque KOUTONIN, (Tuesday, January 28th, 2014) http://www.siliconafrica.com/france-colonial-tax/

Table of Abbreviations

AU   African Union

OAU   Organization of African Unity

PIP   Proper-integration procedure

FOCAC

IDEAS

IMF

NO

US

Key words; *Africa, West, Politics, Underdevelopment, Poverty, Misery, Violent, Liberty, Continent, China, Europeans, 21ˢᵗ Century, History, State, Fragile Corruption, Diplomacy.*

See, Walter Rodney, How Europe underdeveloped Africa, an Introduction by Vincent Harding. 1982, Pp. Xii-xxi,

Key words; *Africa, West, Politics, Underdevelopment, Poverty, Misery, Violent, Liberty, Continent, China, Europeans, 21st Century, History, State, Fragile Corruption, Diplomacy.*

See, the economics, what is wrong with the democracy?
http://www.economist.com/news/essays/21596796-democracy-was-most-successful-political-idea-20th-century-why-has-it-run-trouble-and-what-can-be-do

Printed in Great Britain
by Amazon

55660913R00106